THE DECISIVE INVESTIGATOR

CRIME SCENES, EVIDENCE, AND PROOF.

ERIC GOLEMBIEWSKI

INTRYOLI PRESS

The Decisive Investigator: Crime Scenes, Evidence, and Proof.

ISBN Paperback 978-0-9993151-4-9

First edition, first printing, 2019

Publisher's Cataloging-in-Publication Data

Golembiewski, Eric

The Decisive Investigator: Crime Scenes, Evidence, and Proof. / Eric Golembiewski. – 1st ed.

p. cm.

1. Criminal investigation—Handbooks, manuals, etc. 2. Evidence, criminal—Handbooks, manuals, etc. 3. Crime Scene searches—Handbooks, manuals, etc.

I. Title.

363.25

2019

To the investigators.

CONTENTS

Chapter 3. Evidence Work

INTRODUCTION

The Decisive Investigator: Crime Scenes, Evidence, and Proof shows a method to solve cases with evidence obtained from scenes. The investigator faces four main decisions for any case.

How to organize investigations?

How to work scenes?

How to work evidence?

How to evaluate investigations?

Organization of investigations forms the basis of competent investigation work. All parts of a case's organization require the components of objectivity, facts, direction, and writing. Organization presents the seven different potential emphasis areas in a case. The investigator considers cases from the perspectives of victim, witness, suspect, crime dynamics, law, scene, and evidence. Cases have different emphasis and the investigator's ability to shift between them makes strong cases.

Scenes create and hold the evidence of interactions. Scene investigations require the investigator convert the case to a workable scene, perform scene analysis, and engage the scene to find evidence. Scenes come in five main types of public, private, car, tool, and person.

Evidence proves interactions of scenes. Evidence investigations require the investigator collect, analyze, and convert evidence into proof. Anything can qualify as evidence, but this book refines evidence to six categories most common in investigations as information, photographs, artifacts, biological material, fingerprints, and patterns.

Evaluation of cases helps the investigator know the level of proving who did what for the case, and what to do next. The investigator evaluates the parts of a case with same parts as in the organization including objectivity, facts, direction, and writing. The evaluation looks at the same perspective areas in a case as the organization but based on building the case instead of discovering evidence. The investigator considers scenes, evidence, crime dynamics, victim, witness, suspect, and law.

The four decisions in *The Decisive Investigator* provide a scalable method to solve cases with component decisions to apply to the case situation at hand. The investigator advances the case with the outcomes of each decision by building the body of facts. Facts prove who did what.

CHAPTER 1. INVESTIGATION ORGANIZATION

The decisive investigator applies functional goals as organizing methods for proving who did what. The investigator uses four parts or methods to address the different component investigations in every case: objectivity, proof, direction and writing.

The component investigations cover the common themes in every case: victims, witnesses, suspects, dynamics, laws, scenes, and evidence. These thematic investigations often come in this order to the investigator with each sub investigation building on others.

How to organize an investigation?

The decisive investigator organizes investigations around the four concepts of objectivity, proof, direction, and writing.

Goal. The investigator seeks to define the component and address it with objectivity, facts, direction, and writing.

I. Objectivity

A. Open Mindedness. The investigator accepts a large range of possibilities while avoiding making early and unsupported judgments. Questioning everything and tracing the origin of the ideas helps keep the case to the facts. The investigator also accepts ambiguity as a part of investigation. The early part of an investigation has the broadest spectrum of options.

1. Anything could happen.

2. Any person could do anything with individualized motives and logic.

3. Any scene could have any involvement and hold the key evidence

B. Reasoning. The investigator considers the evidence to convert it to proof and then facts.

1. Every event has a cause and effect with an action and reaction.

2. Deductive reasoning goes from general ideas to specifics. Top down guidance like statistics, conventional wisdom, and experience about investigations provide some good background, but do not solve cases.

3. Inductive reasoning goes from particulars to general ideas. Inductive reasoning uses evidence with a bottom up approach to get to proving points, and establish facts.

4 The investigator recognizes the difference between an observation and an inference. Observation means noting information. Inferences synthesize facts and ideas to build more ideas. Solid inferences built on evidence, proof, and facts, come up with objective ideas. Reasoning prevents runaway open mindedness. The investigator converts direct and indirect evidence into proof, and proof into facts. Faulty thinking delivers the investigation to a destination by a faulty path. A non-fact driven process produces non-factual outcomes. Sometimes a nonobjective process (subjective process) gets lucky and arrives to the correct answer, such as getting the suspect right, but the investigation lacks the means to prove those conclusions.

C. Bias Awareness. The investigator recognizes the threat of bias to investigations. Preconceived ideas sway investigations from the truth. The investigator keeps aware of bias to ensure the logic of the case does not become shaped by preconceived ideas.

1. Dynamic bias applies to a preconceived idea about the possibilities of the actions in a case.

2. Personal bias applies to how an investigator uses preconceived ideas about a person and how those ideas influence how he treats the person.

3. Scene bias applies to a scene's involvement in the case.

4. Evidence bias applies to how the investigator interprets the evidence.

II. Facts

A. Individual. The investigator looks at evidence to prove a particular point. Direct evidence proves a point by itself, while indirect evidence combines conditions together. Individual proof comes in five overlapping capabilities of identification, presence, action, control, and damage.

1. The investigator seeks to prove identification by specifying a particular person, place, artifact, or activity by name, or characteristics.

2. The investigator seeks to prove presence showing how scenes interacted with other scenes.

3. The investigator seeks prove action showing how some scenes took action.

4. The investigator seeks to prove control showing how some scenes controlled other scenes.

5. The investigator seeks prove impact showing how damage, injury, or change resulted from scene interaction.

B. Group. The investigator groups different evidence from a base concept to establish depth of proof and key facts. Base concepts include all presence evidence at one scene, or all evidence showing a connection between to specific scenes, or any specific area of an investigation. The investigator compares parallel evidence for independence, corroboration, or refutation.

1. Independent evidence proves a fact on its own. Some cases only have independent evidence, and the investigator combines independent evidence to prove facts.

2. Corroborating evidence backs up other evidence to prove the same facts.

3. Refuting evidence shows contradictory facts. It calls for more work in corroboration to determine the correct facts, and reasons for outlier facts. The situation could indicate false statements, factual errors, planted evidence, or poor investigator activities. Lack of evidence does not make the evidence adversarial. An investigator omitting adversarial evidence derails a case in court when attorneys call attention to it as a shoddy job, or a deliberate abuse.

C. Collective. The investigator uses critical thinking to gather all evidence from investigative actions to establish culpability by connecting scenes through evidence.

1. Ruling out means the evidence does not support including the activities, scenes, persons, tools, and anything else in a case in a group of possibilities.

2. Ruling in means the evidence supports at least some connection with the crime.

3. Exculpability leads to exoneration by proving a person has no responsibility for a crime, or proves someone else did the crime and clears the person.

4. Culpability leads to charging a person in a court case for a crime by proving the person has responsibility for it.

III. Direction

A. Priorities. The investigator seeks to adhere to the organization of the case, and how to investigate.

1. The investigator seeks to prove who did what through evidence.

2. The investigator seeks to use the four methods of objectivity, proof, direction, and writing to build an investigation formed on solid discipline.

3. The investigator seeks to address specifics with the seven sub-investigations of victims, witnesses, suspects, dynamics, laws, scenes, and evidence for full coverage of the case.

B. Status. The investigator determines the status of the established priorities. The investigator assesses the status of any part on the gaps in evidence, proof, and facts.

1. The investigator meets priorities if able to obtain evidence to prove who did what.

2. The investigator meets some priorities if able to obtain some evidence to prove some facts of the case.

3. The investigator fails to meet priorities if unable obtain evidence to prove the case with the current options. This indicates the investigator will not solve the case.

C. Plans. The investigator compares his actions with the priorities to determine the status and then plans the way forward to close the gaps exposed in the status check.

1. If the investigator meets the priorities of the investigation and can prove who did what, then he sends the case to prosecution.

2. If the investigator meets some of the priorities of the investigation and can prove some facts, then the case requires more work and a list of tasks, or a list of what stands in the way of the investigation. The investigator looks at options to get the case to the goals through evidence, proof, and facts. The lack often points to an area of the investigation in one of the four methods or seven themes.

3. If the investigator finds it impossible to meet the priorities of the investigation and prove some facts, then he will forward the case for review, and probable closing or suspension. If the investigator decides against further action without a return on investment he explains at the end of the report the lack of suspects and leads causing him to close or inactivate the case.

IV. Writing

A. Format. Organizing the case report presents it in usable form for others. The format of the writing in a case arranges the order of processes with attention to chronology within parts. The investigator covers the case by organizing the report in a logical order, making facts easy to find.

1. Synopsis sections summarize what happened and the investigator actions with an informal dozen sentences or fragmentary expressions using passive verbiage to give a quick rundown of the case.

2. Participants or the PLEO (Participating Law Enforcement Officers) name the personnel who worked on the case.

3. Notification sections cover the role of the investigator, how the case came to his attention, and the specific dates and times.

4. Statement sections cover who said what to the investigator as part of the informational evidence.

5. Scene descriptions describe what the investigator observed including appearances and measurements. The investigator integrates evidence locations into the description to build understanding of the relationship between evidence. The investigator describes scene details in sharp focus with plain language to make them clear to an outsider reading the case. The investigator's narrative covers the details beyond departmental computer forms to collect searchable data such as biographical information on involved persons, places, cars, evidence, and outcomes.

6. Evidence sections organize the evidence by type, location, chronology, law violation, or process, depending on which makes more sense to the person writing the case. The report covers all of the evidence types if only to note the attempt. The absence of evidence attempts looks partial or incompetent.

7. Activity sections cover what persons did during the course of the crime.

8. Charging sections explain law by breaking them down into specific elements. Sometimes investigators add the suspect's specific actions to the elements if the law has complicated parts.

9. Status sections cover the status of various components of the investigation. The investigator also covers where he processed evidence and include the scene status. Suspect status tells the reader how close the case comes to proving the allegations against a particular person.

10. Sketches sometimes cover information better than words alone. Investigators document important locations on a person's body by creating sketches. Some departments have blank sketches available, or the investigator finds them on the internet. The investigator avoids duplicating medical examiner processes with dead bodies or sexual assault case, recognizing the physician has control over the scene and greater expertise in the field. Basic observations and measurements provide enough information to work the case.

11. The investigator may need to include a process map of how the device works to help understand the complex aspects of a person uses an information tool in a crime.

B. Descriptions. The investigator's report describes things with accuracy and methodology to create a mental picture of scenes, evidence, and actions, and also includes attributes of origin, ownership, location, and relationships. The investigator also includes sensory observations in descriptions when they distinguish the subject. Descriptions use common language and avoid police jargon to facilitate understanding.

C. Grammar. Good sentences build good reports. The investigator does this by having a solid understanding of how to use parts of the language in order to express the case. Sometimes fragments cover more information faster without sacrificing details.

1. Nouns include the subject and objects of the report. Proper nouns provide

maximum specificity. Nonspecific pronouns cause confusion. The investigator should only use *they* or *them* to indicate plural persons.

2. Adjectives modify nouns, and they help to make descriptions more specific. A *red car* provides a smaller group of possible cars than a *car*. The investigator also clarifies information in the report by limiting adjective use to describe situations and things with objective observations. *An angry man* provides no support for the conclusion of anger.

3. Verbs in the active form best show the actions of the sentences. Sentence structure with active verbs follow the format of the subject did a particular action to the object such as, *I took fingerprints*. Passive form verbs complicate messages when they make the object (receiver) the center of the sentence in place of the subject (doer). This style expresses the sentence as an action happened to a subject such as, *fingerprints were taken*, or the *fingerprints were taken by the man*. The passive form requires more work to read as it presents words in odd syntax backwards, and omits key information about the subject, and disrupts the reader trying to determine who did the action. Passive verbs turn an action into a (passive) state of being. The verb *to be* provides a less accurate description of actions instead of a more accurate form of verb to explain what happened. *I collected fingerprints*, presents a single direct action instead of a state of being in, *I was collecting fingerprints*. The first sentence expresses action, but the second bloats the sentence, expressing the action as a state of being. Situations change over time, and past tense specifies details as they were instead of as they are.

4. Adverbs modify verbs, adjectives, and other adverbs to tell how, when, where, why, or how often. They often end in *ly*. *I liberally applied fingerprint powder to the window,* describes how *I applied fingerprint powder,* but liberally does not make it any clearer by using an unnecessary word. Word combinations like to *yell angrily*, or *run quickly* also embed a conclusion more than an observation. Documenting the facts explains details, such as, *the man clenched his fists when talking,* and *I observed his red face, and veins in his neck.*

5. Contractions like *didn't*, have limited acceptable uses for statements, but their informality and lack of precision with negatives creates confusion.

6 Apostrophe use confuses readers when a writer misuses them to distinguish possession, contraction, and plurals, and their positioning matters. The phrase *the dog's paws* refers to a single dog possessing paws. *The dogs' paws,* refers to multiple dogs possessing their own paws.

D. Style. Direct language with crisp, informative, and solid sentences transfers case knowledge best. The report sections provide an orderly chronological presentation of events. If the case goes to court, the report acts as the investigator's summarized statement for testimony.

1.1 ORGANIZING VICTIM INVESTIGATIONS

Most cases open with a victim and a perceived crime against the victim. Victim investigations connect persons or organizations as scenes to actions. Cases have victims of persons, businesses, organizations, or governments. The victim exists as a scene and a self-directed thinking entity with several scenes under control.

Goal. The investigator seeks to define the victim, the victim's actions, and how the suspect impacted the victim with the crime.

I. Objectivity

A. Open Mindedness. The investigator considers alternate ideas and courses for the designated victim. Cases can have more than one victim with persons rotating between roles of victims, witnesses, and suspects over the course of time and in different cases. The investigator obtains more evidence by considering most victims have an active role in cases, instead of passive receivers of suspect actions. The investigator documents victims' actions, imperfections, mistakes and crimes without emotion guided by evidence and proof.

B. Reasoning. The investigator approaches the victim with logical thinking and inductive reasoning processes to collect particular facts in order to arrive at a provable victim. Victim investigations parallel suspect investigations, and come with a host of subordinate scenes.

C. Bias Awareness. The investigator recognizes potential bias when speaking with a victim or someone advocating on his or her behalf. Cooperating serves the victim's interests to recover from the damage. The first person an investigator speaks with has a greater chance of legitimizing his or her version of event. Investigators meet victims first, which can bias the investigator toward treating the victim's version of events as the official one. The wronged party can trigger sympathetic emotions in the investigator. Focusing on collecting evidence and avoiding counseling victims reduces bias, making decisions easier.

II. Facts

A. Individual. Victim investigations look at the outcome of how the victim acted in the case, producing evidence showing those interactions. The investigator defines the victim by evidence to address the five proof types. Victim evidence has an origin and discovery location, so victim evidence has a suspect component as a part of it.

1. Identification evidence proves the identity of the victim as a specific person.

2. Presence evidence proves a victim scene interacted with other scenes.

3. Action evidence proves a victim scene took actions with another scene and contributed to the events connected with the crime.

4. Control evidence proves a victim had involvement with another scene by taking or losing possession.

5. Impact evidence proves how the victim scene received damage or injury during the course of interactions. Victims inflict damage or injury on other scenes in the course of the crimes also.

B. Group. The investigator groups different evidence from a base concept of the victim to establish depth of proof and key facts. The investigator compares parallel evidence for independence, corroboration, or refutation.

1. Independent evidence proves a fact about the victim on its own.

2. Corroborating evidence validates facts about the victim by using different evidence to prove the same facts in a base concept.

3. Refuting evidence shows adversarial about the victim to establish different theories about victim activities. Some victims lie about their involvement or provide statements with unintentional errors, or imprecise facts.

C. Collective. The investigator looks at the total body of evidence in a case to connect the victim to his activities and determine culpability.

1. Ruling out means the collective evidence does not support the possibility a victim has responsibility for a crime.

2. Ruling in means the collective evidence supports the possibility a victim has responsibility for a crime.

3. Exculpability evidence clears victims by proving a person has no responsibility for a crime.

4. Culpability leads to charging a person in a court case for a crime by proving the person has responsibility for it. Culpability makes a person the suspect.

III. Direction

A. Priorities. The investigator's priorities for the victim centers on connecting the person scene and his actions to other scenes by evidence. The investigator uses evidence to connect the victim to the outcome or fruits of the crime.

1. The investigator seeks to the victim.

2. The investigator seeks to use the four methods to work on the victim part of the case.

3. The investigator seeks to work on the victim sub investigation by also working on the other six themes.

B. Status. The investigator assesses the facts supporting the victim's role, and determines the gaps.

1. The investigator meets priorities if able to obtain evidence to prove what each victim did for the case.

2. The investigator meets priorities in part if able to obtain evidence to prove some facts about what each victim did for the case.

3. The investigator fails to meet priorities if unable to obtain evidence to prove what each victim did for the case.

C. Plans. The investigator plans the next step with the victim given the current status.

1. If the investigator meets the priorities of the victim investigation then the investigator has finished it, and sends the case on.

2. If the investigator meets some of the priorities of the victim investigation and can prove some facts, then the case requires more work.

3. If the investigator fails to meet the priorities of the victim investigation and prove some facts, then he will forward the case to another entity.

IV. Writing

A. Format. The investigator organizes the victim report in a logical order, making facts easy to find with four parts: identifying the person, describing the person's actions, explaining the outcome, and reporting the victim's statement.

B. Descriptions. The investigator describes the victim in detail, and the outcome the victim experienced with plain language. The victim's physical description goes from the head to the feet. The investigator's description of the victim expands to cover subordinate scenes like cars and tools.

C. Grammar. The investigator makes the victim as a person and his actions clear by using proper nouns and active language to cover the suspect.

D. Style. The investigator's writing about the victim covers the details in a neutral manner similar to suspect coverage.

1.2 ORGANIZING WITNESS INVESTIGATIONS

Witnesses come first or second in the investigator's contacts, sometimes before incapacitated or absent victims. The witness exists as a scene and a self-directed thinking entity having observed events to connect scenes, actions, and evidence to each other.

Goal. The investigator seeks to define the witness as an observer, the witness's actions, and what the witness can contribute to the facts about the case.

I. Objectivity

A. Open Mindedness. The investigator considers witness statements and their leads to evidence for alternate ideas and courses of action.

B. Reasoning. The investigator approaches the witness and evidence with logical thinking aimed at proving ideas. They provide specific evidence points and particulars the investigator can use with inductive reasoning toward proving facts. Witnesses can give inaccurate or wrong information, but they tend to provide more objective information when they have less invested in the outcome of the case.

C. Bias Awareness. The investigator investigates the witness in a neutral, fact finding way like the suspect and victim, and should weigh the information and articulable facts to avoid bias for or against the witness. Witnesses range from neutral to suspect or victim loyal. The ideal witness provides evidence with no connection to anyone else in the case, provides a detailed account of events, and assists the investigator in finding evidence with little to gain or lose.

II. Facts

A. Individual. The witness evidence relates to limited parts of the activity, providing limited proof among the five options. The witness provides guidance to find evidence in other places in addition to details about activities.

1. Identification evidence defines the witness, and whatever he brings forth by proof, and any connections with other persons in the case.

2 Presence evidence proves the witness's presence to the events by proximity, position, and relationship to the relevant evidence as well as proving the presence of the witness's evidence.

3. Action evidence proves the witness's actions to observe the other scenes and evidence, and the actions alleged by the witness.

4. Control evidence proves what the witness controlled, and any control activities or involved entities the witness alleged.

5. Impact evidence proves the damage or injury of the crime as stated by the witness.

B. Group. The investigator compares witness evidence from the same scene to corroborate facts with consistent proof, or discover discrepancies.

1. Independent witness evidence proves a fact about the entities or activities the witness described without corroboration.

2. Corroborating evidence validates facts originating from the witness by using different evidence to prove the same facts. Sometimes the witness evidence corroborates other witness evidence or involved parties.

3. Refuting evidence shows countering witness evidence based facts.

C. Collective. The investigator looks at the total body of witness evidence in a case to connect scenes and determine what facts the witness adds to support or weaken culpability.

1. Ruling out means the witness evidence does not support the possibility a person has responsibility for a crime.

2. Ruling in means the witness evidence supports the possibility a person has responsibility for a crime.

3. Exculpability indicates the witness evidence clears a person of having responsibility for activities.

4. Culpability indicates the witness evidence proves a person has responsibility for activities by using the evidence to connect several scenes together forming a chain from suspect to victim.

III. Direction

A. Priorities. The investigator prioritizes witness investigation on obtaining information leading to evidence. The investigator evaluates the witness's involvement in the case, how well the evidence shows the person's role, what the evidence stemming from the witness proves, and what the investigator needs to do next.

1. The investigator seeks to obtain witness evidence to prove who did what.

2. The investigator seeks to investigate the witness with the four methods.

3. The investigator seeks to support the victim sub investigation with the six other thematic investigations.

B. Status. The investigator assesses the witness evidence for what it proves. Multiple witnesses complicate status assessments with unstructured data from different sources.

1. The investigator meets priorities if able to obtain evidence to prove what the witness reported about the case.

b. The investigator meets priorities in part if able to obtain evidence to prove some facts about what each witness reported about the case.

c. The investigator fails to meet priorities if unable to obtain evidence to prove what each witness reported about the case.

C. Plans. The investigator plans the next step with the witness given the current status. The investigator re-interviews the witness to fill gaps.

1. If the investigator meets the priorities of the witness investigation then the investigator has finished it, and sends the case on.

b. If the investigator meets some of the priorities of the witness investigation and can prove some facts, then the case requires more work.

c. If the investigator finds it impossible to meet the priorities of the witness investigation and prove some facts, then he will forward the case to another entity.

IV. Writing

A. Format. The investigator covers the witness by organizing the report in a logical order, making facts easy to find. The witness section identifies the person, the person's connections with the case and persons, and describes what the person observed including the evidence.

B. Descriptions. The investigator describes the witness in detail, and what the person brings to the case. A physical description, head to toe, like suspects or victims, helps with cross referencing. The investigator includes what the witness observed, and relevant measurements or estimates about the situation such as how he saw things, under what condition, and from what distance.

C. Grammar. The investigator uses specific language with proper nouns and active verbs to write about the witness.

D. Style. The investigator's writing about the witness covers the person and what the person knows leading to evidence. The investigator writes about the witness with factual neutrality in a clear first person style covering the facts in an informational style with quotes capture the exact words. The investigator clarifies points in the statement to make it as specific as possible.

1.3 ORGANIZING SUSPECT INVESTIGATIONS

All investigations define the suspect as the person accused of the crime with supporting evidence connecting persons as scenes to actions. The suspect themed investigation comes third, building on the victim and witness even if the suspect remains an abstract concept.

Goal. The investigator seeks to define the suspect, the suspect's actions, and how the suspect impacted the victim by the crime.

I. Objectivity

A. Open Mindedness. Anyone has the capability to commit a crime, and fill the role of suspect including man, woman, young, old, beautiful, ugly, respected, or reviled. Suspects also have a spectrum of abilities, skills, and competence connected with the ability to stay on task, or change course. The investigator considers alternate suspects and courses of action for a case with multiple suspects. The US Constitution deems suspects innocent until proven guilty in a court of law. No matter what the investigator thinks, the law sees the suspect as innocent until the courts decide otherwise.

B. Reasoning. The investigator approaches the suspect with logical thinking focused on proving facts through evidence. The investigator uses an inductive approach to defining the suspect by collecting particular facts to name a suspect. The investigator remembers the job requires obtaining facts, not counseling. Those facts come with reasons and excuses, and the investigator parses out the proof and facts from opinions.

C. Bias Awareness. The investigator recognizes bias surrounding investigating a person as a suspect as a threat to neutral, thorough, and high quality decisions. The investigator overcomes bias by focusing on open mindedness, fact based thinking, and reasoning. An investigator can have a natural tendency of hostility toward a suspect with a more gruesome, heinous, or sexual crime.

II. Facts

A. Individual. The investigator looks at suspect evidence in the five varieties to develop the case.

1. Identification evidence proves the identity of the suspect. Only cases with an identifiable suspect go to court, those with unidentified suspects still advance the case or help with different cases.

2. Presence evidence proves a suspect scene interacted with other scenes, placing him at the scene.

3. Action evidence proves a suspect scene took actions to further the crime.

4. Control evidence proves a suspect had involvement with another scene by taking or losing possession.

5. Impact evidence proves how the suspect scene damaged or injured other scenes or received damage or injury during the course of interactions. *Corpus delecti* evidence proves the crime happened.

B. Group. The investigator looks at different evidence types from the base concept of the suspect for corroboration.

1. Independent evidence proves a fact without corroboration about the suspect and his activities.

2. Corroborating evidence validates facts about the suspect by using different evidence to prove the same facts in a base concept.

3. Refuting evidence shows countering suspect facts. The investigator includes inconsistent evidence in the report to ensure it has all the proof and facts leading to fair decisions about suspects.

C. Collective. The investigator looks at the total body of evidence in a case to determine the suspect's level of culpability. The courts decide guilt or innocence, but the investigator looks at the collective facts connecting the suspect to the victim to decide if a person has responsibility for a crime by evidence connecting multiple scenes together. Cases being with the investigator ruling suspects in or out, and advance to their exculpability and culpability.

1. Ruling out means the collective evidence does not support the possibility a person has responsibility for a crime. Some cold cases loop around to focus on suspects the investigators ruled out early when they lacked evidence to connect the scenes.

2. Ruling in means the collective evidence supports the possibility a person has responsibility for a crime. If someone dies at a party the investigator rules everyone in at first.

3. Exculpability indicates the suspect does not have responsibility for activities. This happens when some fact indicates a different chain from the victim to a different suspect, exonerating a suspect. Defense attorneys always look for exculpatory evidence to prove their clients did not commit a crime. They also look for indications the investigator failed to include exculpatory evidence about their client to exonerate him. An attorney's claims of evidence with exculpatory features, along with investigator misconduct can ruin a case.

4. Culpability indicates evidence forms a chain connecting a suspect to the victim and other scenes proving responsibility for activities. The investigator provides evidence of the mens rea, (mindset of the suspect), the actus reus, (criminal act), as well as the corpus delecti, (body of evidence) to prove the suspect intended to commit a crime, and did so.

III. Direction

A. Priorities. The investigator's first priority for the suspect centers on connecting the person scene and his actions to other scenes by evidence to prove guilt or innocence.

1. The investigator seeks to investigate the suspect and prove who did what by examining the most suspect connected scene available.

2. The investigator looks at the six other themes of investigations to support the suspect investigation.

3. The investigator uses the four methods to build the case about the suspect.

B. Status. The investigator assesses if the investigation meets the parameters for investigating the suspect by considering the provable facts of the case, determining what laws the suspect violated for charging in court.

1. The investigator meets priorities if able to obtain evidence to prove what each suspect did for the case, and how he connects with other scenes, evidence, and dynamics.

2. The investigator meets priorities in part if able to obtain evidence to prove some facts about what each suspect did for the case.

3. The investigator fails to meet priorities if unable to obtain evidence to prove what each suspect did for the case.

C. Plans. The investigator knows the next step with the suspect given the current status. The investigator plans how to expand the evidence by more interviews, or expansion to other scenes. The investigator lines up the evidence for an identified suspect to prepare for charging a person if a break comes later. John Doe warrants identify a suspect by a person's DNA profile, and increase chances of solving the cases over time with an unnamed suspect. The warrant converts what was an unknown suspect who might outlast the statute of limitations on a crime into an identified fugitive.

1. If the investigator meets the priorities of the suspect investigation then the investigator has finished it, and sends the case on.

2. If the investigator meets some of the priorities of the suspect investigation and can prove some facts, then the case requires more work.

3. If the investigator finds it impossible to meet the priorities of the suspect investigation and prove some facts, then he will forward the case to another entity.

IV. Writing

A. Format. The investigator covers the suspect by organizing the report in a logical order, making facts easy to find. Suspect sections of reports focus on describing the suspect, detailing his actions, explaining the outcomes of those actions, and covering his statements.

B. Descriptions. The investigator describes the suspect in detail with plain language from the head to the feet., covering key parts and including other sensory observations. Some person descriptions expand to cover subordinate scenes the suspect used as extensions of his person, such as cars and tools.

C. Grammar. The investigator use proper nouns and adjectives along with active verbs to describe the suspect and his actions with precision.

D. Style. The investigator writes about the suspect with factual neutrality in a clear first person style covering the facts to make clear the origins of the facts used in the investigation into the suspect. The term Defendant applies in court and the District Attorney designates the person.

1.4 ORGANIZING CRIME DYNAMIC INVESTIGATIONS

Cases have dynamic activity connecting all the entities. Dynamics investigations connect evidence to show the actions among the involved persons and scenes.

Goal. The investigator seeks to define the dynamics of the case as cause and effect activity.

I. Objectivity

A. Open Mindedness. Crime dynamics make almost anything possible, and persons do things for many reasons, along with making mistakes, and changing course along the way. Persons also have different levels of competence in their efforts effecting how the crime turns out. The investigator has to recognize crime as a deviance from the norm and common sense ideas about a person's motives and actions fails to cover the greater spectrum of possible causes and effects.

B. Reasoning. Events unfold and one leads to the other, so the investigator must find the logic strain in what happened. Every case has three stages: preparation, the event, and recovery, each including their own dynamics. A timeline of events help reason the case by conceptualizing what happened when. The investigator working as an early responder faces the temptation of looking at a modus operandi or how the suspect operated, but conducting an investigation adhering to facts advances the case more than theories about actions.

C. Bias Awareness. Investigators narrow down the possibilities of what could happen but they should avoid external based ideas as proof for the crime dynamics.

II. Facts

A. Individual. The investigator shows how the crime dynamics are made of individual facts.

1. Identification evidence identifies activities.

2. Presence evidence proves contact.

3. Action evidence proves the dynamic activities.

4. Control evidence proves how a scene took dynamic steps to control or possess other scenes.

5. Impact evidence proves the outcome of the dynamics.

B. Group. The investigator looks at different evidence types about the dynamics for independence, corroboration, or refutation.

1. Independent evidence proves a fact about a specific dynamic in the chain of actions.

2. Corroborating evidence validates facts about dynamics to prove the same facts in a base concept.

3. Refuting evidence shows countering facts about the dynamics.

C. Collective. The investigator looks at the total body of evidence in a case to show culpability for crime dynamics by proof of evidence.

1. Ruling out means the collective evidence does not support the possibility of a person's involvement in the crime dynamics.

2. Ruling in means at least some of the collective evidence supports the possibility of a person's involvement in the crime dynamics.

3. Exculpability evidence proves a person not responsible for crime dynamics.

4. Culpability evidence proves a person responsible for crime dynamics.

III. Direction

A. Priorities. The investigator connects crime dynamics with specific persons by proving it with evidence.

1. The investigator seeks to prove the dynamics in the case as they fit into who did what.

2. The investigator seeks to incorporate the four methods into the case dynamics.

3. The investigator seeks to prove the case dynamics with evidence showing how the dynamics incorporate the six other themes of the investigation.

B. Status. The investigator determines how much the evidence supports the dynamics.

1. The investigator meets priorities if able to obtain evidence to prove the dynamics.

2. The investigator meets priorities in part if able to obtain evidence to prove some facts about how the scenes and evidence participate in the dynamics.

3. The investigator fails to meet priorities if unable to obtain evidence to prove the dynamics.

C. Plans. The investigator decides how to address the status of the dynamics.

1. If the investigator meets the priorities of proving the dynamics he sends the finished case on.

2. If the investigator meets some of the priorities of the dynamics and can prove some facts, then the case requires more work.

3. If the investigator finds it impossible to meet the priorities of the dynamics, then he will forward the case to another entity either as a closed case, or one needing more work.

IV. Writing

A. Format. The investigator writes about the dynamics by making them readable in the report. Actions beget other actions, so the investigator reports them in chronological order by person who did the actions.

B. Descriptions. The investigator often describes the dynamics in detail in the section about the person who did them. Sometimes a witness describes the dynamics about other persons. Evidence indicates dynamics.

C. Grammar. The investigator uses proper nouns, specific adjectives, and active verbs to express clear sentences about what happened.

D. Style. The investigator writes about the crime dynamics to explain how they work in simple form incorporating evidence, proof, and facts into the sections.

1.5 ORGANIZING LAW INVESTIGATIONS

An investigation connects entities and activities to law violations by evidence. This book approaches the application of the law as dynamic, where the suspicion of a violation triggers the investigation, and it builds support or not from there. It also takes the case to the level of a jury trial, beyond the probable cause standard to arrest a person.

Goal. The investigator defines the law violations by connecting them with evidence to scenes, evidence, a victim, and a suspect.

I. Objectivity

A. Open Mindedness. The investigator looks at many different laws to explore their application to the case. Facts become available as the case progresses. Sometimes the investigator uncovers new violations, or realizes the actions fit different violations. Laws provide the framework of elements, or conditions to prove. An investigator recognizes a law violation before having the evidence to prove it. The average suspect commits multiple law violations during the course of a crime.

B. Reasoning. The investigator approaches laws with logical thinking about evidence, provable points, and facts. Authorities create laws with a general idea of a violation comprised of three or four required elements. Investigators use inductive reasoning to show how the particular facts fit with the law. Law objectivity requires the investigator know the law and apply it to make the law fit the facts. There are thousands of laws stemming from four basic laws of assault, burglary, theft, and order. The investigator should know how the four work as the key to understanding the others.

1. Assault. A person assaults another by violating the person with physical force or fear. Examples include homicide, kidnapping, and rape.

2. Burglary. A person commits burglary by breaking into the building of another with intent to commit a crime inside. Examples include break-ins, robberies, and home invasion robberies.

3. Theft. A person commits theft by taking the property of another. Examples include shoplifting, what people think of as burglary, and car theft.

4. Order. A family of laws center on keeping safety and order by outlawing dangerous and unruly acts. Examples include drug possession, driving under the influence, and speeding.

C. Bias Awareness. The investigator recognizes bias related to persons subject to the law, and takes steps to apply the law with fairness using facts. Sometimes the investigator takes a moral approach lacking synchronization with the law. When officers identify cases by the law violation before knowing the details it creates expectations about the crime type, and colors what they search for, and what they do not. Some investigators have a bias for anticipating how the court case proceeds, such as an incompetent suspect, or juvenile suspect leading to a lower standard.

II. Facts.

A. Individual. The investigator knows the laws applicable to the case, and how to prove them with the facts.

1. Identification evidence identifies scenes entities and actions involved in a law violation.

2. Presence evidence shows scene presence with others relating to law violations.

3. Action evidence proves a person took particular actions with matters in a particular place and time.

4. Control evidence proves how scenes controlled or possessed other scenes and actions to break the law.

5. Impact evidence proves the outcome of the broken law resulting in damage or injury. The *corpus delecti* proves a crime occurred, and the investigator finds it among the individual proof.

B. Group. The investigator looks at different evidence types from the base concept of the law violations for corroboration through consistent proof or not about entities and activities. The investigator seeks to analyze law evidence for its independence, corroboration, or refutation.

1. Independent evidence proves a fact about a law violation without corroboration about entities and activities.

2. Corroborating evidence validates facts about entities and activities relating to law violations by using different evidence to prove the same facts in a base concept.

3. Refuting evidence shows countering facts relating to law violations about different evidence pieces.

C. Collective. The investigator looks at the total body of evidence in a case to determine proximity to culpability for a law violation by proof of evidence.

1. Ruling out means none of the collective evidence supports the possibility of a law violation.

2. Ruling in means at least some of the collective evidence supports the possibility of a law violation. The outset of investigations rule in law violations as the investigator seeks evidence to prove them.

3. Exculpability evidence proves an entity or activity not responsible for a law violation.

4. Culpability evidence proves an entity or activity responsible for at least some aspect of breaking a law or by meeting every condition of the law. Legal culpability requires the parts the mens rea, actus reus, and habeas corpus.

a. Mens rea. The mens rea means the person must have a criminal intent to commit a crime.

b. Actus reus. The actus reus means act must have an objective element of a crime.

c. Habeas corpus. The crime must have a body of evidence.

III. Direction

A. Priorities. The investigator seeks to connect law violations with specific persons and prove it with evidence.

1. The investigator seeks to understand the law's conditions and requirements to prove who did what.

2. The investigator seeks to use the four methods to maximize all applicable law violations to build a robust case.

3. The investigator seeks to connect the six other themed sub investigations to the law violations.

B. Status. The investigator determines how much the evidence supports law violations.

1. The investigator meets priorities if able to obtain evidence to prove who broke what laws.

2. The investigator meets priorities in part if able to obtain evidence to prove some facts about who broke what laws.

3. The investigator fails to meet priorities if unable to obtain evidence to prove who broke what laws.

C. Plans. The investigator decides about charging a person for violating a law, or perhaps a nonspecific person such as an unknown suspect. The investigator also has to decide what to do next to close the gaps discovered in the status of the law investigation.

1. If the investigator meets the priorities of the law investigation then the investigator has finished it, and sends the case on to the next level for prosecution.

2. If the investigator meets some of the priorities of the law investigation and can prove some facts, then the case requires more work.

3. If the investigator finds it impossible to meet the priorities of the law investigation and prove some facts, then he will forward the case to another entity.

IV. Writing

A. Format. The investigator writes about the laws by making the law readable in the report. Laws have elements or conditions a suspect must meet for an investigator to charge the person with a crime. The investigator covers each element, referring to evidence if necessary.

B. Descriptions. The investigator describes the violations in detail while adding in the facts to describe how someone broke the laws.

C. Grammar. The investigator uses proper nouns, specific adjectives, and active verbs to express clear sentences about what happened and the law violation.

D. Style. The investigator writes about laws in simple form by removing the legalese and explaining the law in the simplest of terms to show how the actions fit the crime.

1.6 ORGANIZING SCENE INVESTIGATIONS

Scenes include any physical thing, only differentiated by scale and function. Every physical entity or scene in a case has the potential to create and hold evidence. Scenes come after the involved persons, the laws, and dynamics as they hold the evidence from interactions. Scene investigations provide evidence to prove cases and come before evidence.

Goal. The investigator seeks to define the scenes, and how the interacted to produce evidence.

I. Objectivity

A. Open Mindedness. The investigator looks at all the available scenes, recognizing each scene's uniqueness in creating and holding evidence.

B. Reasoning. The investigator sees scene interactions as a scientific process producing evidence. The investigator uses deductive reasoning to think about how a scene works in general when looking for particular details, but switches to inductive reasoning to combine evidence and understand the overall facts of the scene. The investigator must understand spatial literacy as in how parts of a scene fit together.

C. Bias Awareness. The investigator recognizes bias as a threat to how he chooses and looks at the scene. Bias also colors how he works the scene, and what he obtains from it.

II. Facts

A. Individual. The investigator examines each piece of evidence from the scenes for its unique ability to prove facts. The facts come from all scene types, but persons may provide the best connecting evidence. The investigator seeks all types of proof for a case to show the origin and destination of evidence. If the investigator identifies one scene and evidence, he may use those two to determine the other scene.

1. Identification evidence proves the identity of scenes connected with the case by role, location, and dimensions.

2. Presence evidence proves interactions between scenes.

3. Action evidence proves specific actions by scenes.

4. Control evidence proves possession or control by one scene of another.

5. Impact evidence proves one or more scenes damaged, injured, or impacted another during a crime interaction.

B. Group. The investigator looks at different evidence types from the base concept of a scene for corroboration through consistent proof and inconsistencies. The investigator analyzes scene evidence for its independence, corroboration, or refutation.

1. Independent evidence proves a fact about a scene or transference between scenes without corroboration about entities and activities.

2. Corroborating evidence validates facts about a scene or transference between scenes by using different evidence to prove the same facts in a base concept.

3. Refuting evidence shows countering facts about a scene or evidence transference between scenes.

C. Collective. The investigator looks at the total body of evidence in a case to determine culpability for a law violation. Culpability comes from the investigator's ability to use evidence to connect a string of scenes.

1. Ruling out means none of the evidence supports the possibility of a scene's involvement.

2. Ruling in means at least some of the evidence supports the possibility of a scene's involvement.

3. Exculpability evidence proves a scene or activity from a scene not responsible.

4. Culpability evidence proves a scene responsible for some aspect of the case.

III. Direction

A. Priorities. The investigator seeks central scenes having heavy interactions with other scenes to obtain evidence. Ruined evidence proves nothing. The scene's vulnerability and fragile parts increase its priority. Working a mediocre scene early provides more evidence than holding out for an unavailable great scene.

1. The investigator seeks to prove who did what by investigating the case activity with the most connected scene available, and maximize scene connections.

2. The investigator seeks to investigate the scenes with the four methods for how they connect.

3. The investigator seeks to investigate the scenes' connection with the six other themed sub investigations.

B. Status. The investigator understands the outcomes of scene choice and evidence work in the scene.

1. The investigator meets priorities if able to obtain evidence to prove what each scene did for the case.

2. The investigator meets priorities in part if able to obtain evidence to prove some facts about what each scene did for the case.

3. The investigator fails to meet priorities if unable to obtain evidence to prove what each scene did for the case.

C. Plans. The investigator knows the next step with scenes given the current status and decides if the investigation requires more work with which additional scenes.

1. If the investigator meets the priorities of the scene investigation then the investigator has finished, and sends the case on.

2. If the investigator meets some of the priorities of the scene investigation and can prove some facts, then the case requires more work. Sometimes an investigator takes a fresh try at a new scene with more options than the investigator realize. With no other scenes available to investigate, the investigator expands the scenes he already investigated. The investigator can zoom in, making subscenes their own scenes.

3. If the investigator finds it impossible to meet the priorities of the scene investigation and prove some facts, then he will forward the case to another entity.

IV. Writing

A. Format. The investigator covers the scenes by organizing the report in a logical order, making facts easy to find. The investigator describes the scene, and then covers the evidence by type. Another possible format integrates evidence locations into the descriptions.

B. Descriptions. Scene descriptions focus on how the scene looks, what happened in relation to it, and how it changed. The investigator describes scenes with an overall description, intermediate giving some details, and close descriptions covering details of key components. The investigator describes scenes in detail with plain language including all relevant sensory observations including smells and textures. Scene coverage progresses from one point to another, outside the scene, and moving in. It covers a view of the periphery, ways to get into the scene, and the layout inside the scene. Scene interiors have component parts like the center of gravity, transit paths, and staging areas sometimes requiring descriptions down to the fine details. Scene descriptions contain evidence by location.

Photographs augment scene writing to maximize effective writing. The investigator still includes details if they seem obvious when viewing images. Sketches help explain the scene to readers with key measurements and orientations to show distances and spatial relationships between evidence items and the structures. Sketches can also show how the scene construction influences the actions of persons, like funneling movement.

C. Grammar. The investigator uses language including proper nouns, proper verb tenses, and active language to discuss the scenes with precision.

D. Style. The investigator writes about scenes with concise, detailed descriptions while keeping to the facts in a clear first person style covering the scene in a flowing manner. He attributes as much as possible to each scene by noting ownership, possession, and connections.

1.7 ORGANIZING EVIDENCE INVESTIGATIONS

All investigations define the evidence as the basis to prove facts about a crime. Evidence investigations connect scenes, actions, and people to each other, and form the decisive point of the case. Evidence proves facts, and the investigator investigates the evidence obtained from the scenes. Direct evidence proves an obvious fact and indirect evidence contributes conditional facts used with other facts.

Goal. The investigator seeks to obtain evidence from the scenes to prove who did what.

I. Objectivity

A. Open Mindedness. The investigator locates, collects, and interprets evidence with plural ideas including alternate theories. Premature conclusions cause other evidence to go uncollected, and unanalyzed.

B. Reasoning. The investigator approaches the evidence with logical thinking using deductive reasoning to take the general ideas about evidence and extrapolate the particulars such as scrutinizing common interaction points. The investigator also uses inductive reasoning to go from the particulars of evidence and proof to come up with general ideas as covered in the proof section. Conclusions without supporting evidence damage the investigation and a faulty conclusion makes an opinion instead of a fact.

C. Bias Awareness. The investigator recognizes bias as a threat to understanding evidence capabilities, and takes steps to overcome it. An investigator engages in evidence bias by overestimating what evidence proves and reach for a preformed conclusion, or by ignoring blatant evidence.

II. Facts

A. Individual. Evidence proves specific facts in five different ways by both its origin and discovery scenes.

1. Identification evidence defines a particular person, place, artifact, or activity by name, characteristics, or activity.

2. Presence evidence shows a scene had presence with another scene.

3. Action evidence shows a scene took an action.

4. Control evidence shows a scene controlled another scene.

5. Impact evidence shows a scene impacted another scene.

B. Group. The investigator examines different evidence types as the base concept for proving the case through independent, corroborating, or refuting facts.

1. Independent evidence proves a fact without corroboration although it has a role in proving fact requiring other evidence to prove the fact.

2. Corroborating evidence validates facts with other evidence to prove the same facts in a base concept.

3. Refuting evidence shows countering facts.

C. Collective. The investigator looks at what the total body of evidence in a case proves as facts for culpability by connecting scenes together. Robust evidence showing unique connections provides strong support for culpability, while limited evidence connections provide loose support.

1. Collective evidence unable to support the possibility of assigned responsibility rules out an entity.

2. Collective evidence able to support the possibility of assigned responsibility rules in an entity.

3. Collective evidence able to prove an entity did not have responsibility for activity linking scenes places the entity in the exculpable status.

4. Collective evidence able to prove an entity did have responsibility for activity linking scenes places the entity in the culpable status.

III. Direction

A. Priorities. Evidence makes a case viable, and the investigator obtains evidence to hold persons accountable. The investigator obtains and analyzes evidence considering priorities, status, and plans. The investigator's evidence priorities center on finding, collecting, and keeping it.

1. The investigator seeks to prove who did what by evidence from its origins in scenes.

2. The investigator seeks to investigate the evidence with the four methods.

3. The investigator seeks to maximize evidence connections by cross investigating evidence with the six other themed sub investigations.

B. Status. The investigator assesses how the evidence collected measures against the priorities of proving who did what. The investigator determines what the evidence proves to establish case facts, and the evidence gaps.

1. The investigator meets priorities if able to obtain evidence to prove who did what and all other details about the case.

2. The investigator meets priorities in part if able to obtain evidence to prove some facts through evidence about the case.

3. The investigator fails to meet priorities if unable to obtain evidence to prove who did what in the case.

C. Plans. The investigator determines the next step of what to do by using the assessments to seek out ways to fill the evidence gaps.

1. If the investigator meets the priorities of the evidence investigation then the investigator has finished it, and sends the case on.

2. If the investigator meets some of the priorities of the evidence investigation and can prove some facts, then the case requires more work.

3. If the investigator finds it impossible to meet the priorities of the evidence investigation and prove some facts, then he will forward the case to another entity.

IV. Writing

A. Format. The investigator organizes the coverage of the evidence in the report with a logical order, making facts easy to find. The investigator formats the report to have all evidence of a particular type or process in the same area with locational information on each piece, or cover evidence by location with a separate section on processes.

B. Descriptions. The investigator explains evidence and covers the processes with plain language. Simplification prepares the investigator for an easier time testifying if the case goes to court. The investigator covers the evidence by identifying its location, how the investigator found it, processing to collect it, and chain of custody information. The investigator describes the evidence with precision and accuracy both for it and its location. The investigator documents the chain of custody after seizing the evidence by covering processes, storage locations, and actions with the evidence.

C. Grammar. The investigator uses proper nouns and active verbs to cover the evidence in accurate detail with maximum attribution.

D. Style. The investigator's coverage of the evidence ensures usefulness by covering the facts and their origins. The investigator writes the report to stand in for the evidence, with attention to detail and accuracy.

The investigator writes in the first person style to take the reader on a tour of the evidence. The report covers the evidence in a way to explain the science behind the case.

CHAPTER 2. SCENE WORK

The decisive investigator decides what scene to work, and how to work them by applying functional goals as methods to find the evidence. The investigator uses three parts to look at scenes: case introduction, analyzing scenes, and investigator actions.

The investigator looks eight scene types as components: public, private, car, hand tool, gun, drug, information tool, and person scenes. These thematic component investigations often come in this order as the investigation focuses more on a specific person as the evidence grows.

How to work scenes?

Scene work has a transition from case to scene, analysis, and engagement.

Goal. The investigator seeks to go from responding to a call for service to choosing a scene and investigating the scene for its part in the crime.

I. Case to Scene

A. Presentation. The way a case presents has far reaching implications for the investigation. Cases present in three ways: active, fresh, and delayed.

1. Active. A citizen places a 911 call or the investigator sees a crime in progress for active crime responses.

a. Response. Active scene responses receive lights and sirens from the police and sometimes medics. They cases come with chaos, and the responders first pacify the action, and then organize the investigation. This equates to making many decisions in a short time to help persons and conduct the investigation. Active scene responses provide the investigator the earliest entry into a case and the best access to the scenes and evidence. If the investigator arrives before anyone leaves, then he or she often has the choice of suspect and victim.

b. Scene Options. Many active cases present an ideal situation in a case for securing evidence, however a good portion of them deactivate by the time the investigator gets there. Active scene responses have most of the scenes available.

c. Evidence Considerations. The amount of time, conditions, and accessibility to the scene influences the quality of evidence available to the case. The victim scene and its subordinate scenes, carry much of the evidence proving the case including evidence originating with the suspect. The 911 call includes useful information on the recording, like an eyewitness statement of who did what. Modern 911 systems also capture data of what phone called, making it available for follow up and cell-phone reduces the odds of an anonymous 911 caller.

2. Fresh. Many cases involve fresh responses where crime events recently concluded having no emergency. Fresh scene responses trigger a normal response without lights and sirens.

a. Response. Investigators find fresh responses provide part of the involved parts, reducing choices, but making decisions easier. Fresh responses can present challenges to safety when suspects return to hosting scenes to reignite hostilities. Some family violence cases have both suspect and victim remaining in the hosting scene. When the suspect and victim live together the investigator sees aftershocks with all the chaos in any active case.

b. Scene Options. When the victim or a witness called to report the crime and the suspect had time to flee fresh scene responses provide only some of the scenes by the time the investigator arrives. Fleeing suspects may leave their subscenes behind. On occasion the suspect calls 911 which challenging the investigator to identify and locate the victim half. Witnesses and suspects wanting to avoid speaking with the investigators flee hosting scenes. These incidents rely on a single person's limited perspective statement, but provide more time for the investigator to collect evidence. The scene providing the greatest chance of identifying the suspect presents a good scene to choose. Any scene the suspect interacted with has the potential to provide the evidence of identification and action. Fresh scene response priorities aim toward trying to use the available scenes with a history of suspect interaction to identify the person.

c. Evidence Considerations. Fresh investigations have the potential to have robust evidence even with some of the involved scenes gone.

3. Delayed. Not all persons report crimes in a timely fashion. Some persons wait or are forced to wait to summon an investigator. They may flag down an investigator, approach him in public, or wait in department a lobby to report. Some persons contact an offsite third party, like a supervisor or spouse, who then calls 911. Referrals come to the investigator as delayed reports from an outsider long after the events and without emergency, but can still include major impacts like death.

Schools or social services refer questionable situations to investigators and often have a report to support the referral.

a. Response. An investigator may have to seek an involved person for a delayed response case. Walk-ins bring motivation for an investigation for the investigator to explore by asking why the person walked in instead of calling 911. Sometimes reporting parties choose to walk in for safety reasons. Some potential victims fear an investigation causing more trouble for them, and want to talk about the case with an officer to learn first. Insurance companies suspect late reported accidents for their lack of verification. Referral investigations resemble cold cases, but include crimes in progress like embezzlements. Many jurisdictions have mandated report laws requiring persons who work for medical facilities or schools to report suspected abuse. These cases originate with persons who know the victim and report out of duty. Referrals reach investigators days or weeks after the crime, providing stale and compromised scenes to investigate. Most times someone already cleaned the scene several times. The person bathed, and changed clothes, tainting the scene with a great deal of interactions.

b. Scene Options. Delayed reports create difficulties for scene options. When a person comes to the investigator to report a crime, the person reporting has left the hosting scene unsecured and came to an office to report. When the reporting party has had time to calm down, and the other person has had time to calm down or leave the associated scenes come already pacified. Walk-in investigations come with little or no historical information about the involved entities. The person who walked in occupies the role of center of gravity with evidence of a crime, and provides access to a hosting scene, and other related scenes. Walk-ins present the person and the occasional tool or artifact. The investigator first looks at the scenes the walk-in carried in with him, and soon addresses the rest of the scenes to follow up and establish a link to a suspect scene. Referrals present a difficult set of circumstances to investigate crime scenes challenging the investigator to prove the suspect and victim's identity and status when they have many or no scene connections. Suspect, victim, or witness cooperation leads to access to other scenes, like hosting scenes, and tool scenes such as banking.

c. Evidence Considerations. Walk-ins come with the normal delays plus the delays of a person contacting an investigator beyond the normal time to make the phone call. The reporting party subverts the 911 system, and provides no initial recorded statement. Outside facts from later investigative actions such as an unmentioned custody battle, divorce, or civil problem alter the course of the investigation. Some referral cases victims refuse to cooperate and provide information about the case. They also share information about the case with the suspect, compromising the investigation. On occasion the suspect presents as the victim, or the case revolves around the reporting party using a person painted as a victim to target a person painted as a suspect. Gathering information takes more time when investigator works with difficult persons, reluctant interviewees, or those with diminished capacities. Records have long shelf lives for the investigator to find and analyze. Persons who want an investigation contact the police themselves, and pursue it with enthusiasm. The investigator gains traction by presenting reasons to cooperate to the victims. Referred cases have convoluted parts, making it hard for an investigator to find violations of the law, and evidence to prove it.

B. Investigator Initiation. The investigator initiates the investigation after determining the case origins and accessible connected scenes. The investigator also determines what crimes he suspects connect with the case. By the end of the initiation the investigator should have a rough idea about the investigation. The investigator initiates a case by considering four areas of information: observations, statements, measurements, and history.

1. Observations. The investigator observes details when introduced to a case, seeing the arrangement of scenes, and evidence after the crime. The investigator also sees the outcome of crime. Some citizens compromise the available scenes prior to calling 911 by conducting their own investigation. The investigator documents the specific interferences.

2. Statements. The investigator gains as much information as possible through observation and brief interviews of persons in the area. Who reported the crime, and when he reported it have significance. The investigator meets with the reporting party upon arrival to get a brief statement of what happened, unless he stops an emergency first. The opening statements aid the investigator in determining what crime to investigate, and recognize some of the involved scenes.

Initial statement evidence helps guide investigations to finding the right scenes and evidence within. These factual questions stimulate conversation. Few witnesses answer every question. The investigator asks the same questions from most persons for most crime responses:

Does anyone need medical assistance?

What threats or dangers do you know about?

What crime happened?

What events happened?

Where did it happen?

What did you see?

What did you hear?

Can you describe, recognize, identify, or name the persons involved?

Where did the persons involved go?

What did each person touch during the event, and the times leading up to it, and after?

What outcome resulted from this crime?

The investigator's goal centers on proving who did what, instead of why the person did what. Witnesses provide statements laced with opinions. Persons want to know why an event happened. Reasons, like excuses, come from opinions as much as facts with wide latitude for interpretation. Hate crimes require showing some motivation for the crime as they allege a suspect chose a victim for a reason.

The initial statements set up the investigation, and establish a baseline by covering the generalities of the case: who, what, where, when, and how. Sometimes the investigator only gets the initial statements from a person with no opportunity for follow up, while other times persons consent to provide statements to follow up questions for clarification during or after the evidence collection. The initial statement and what the investigator sees provides him or her with an idea of the five scene types available.

Investigators rely on statements from other investigators in cases, summarizing those statements. The other investigator who made the statement documents the facts in a report to show the origins of the information.

3. Measurements. The investigator has the opportunity to measure parts of the scene in order to specify the scene. Measurements help determine a scene's capabilities.

4. History. Scene ownership and control play key roles in how a case works. Every scene has a history accessible to the investigator in the early phases. Dispatch may provide some background on it, or persons may share what they know.

II. Scene Analysis

A. Physics. Crime scene physics provide the investigator with a group of principles about how scenes create evidence when they interact. Each scene imparts and receives evidence. Some scenes have different physics for different parts.

Evidence flow depends on dynamics, as each scene can act as source or destination for evidence. These abstract rules help the investigator predict how interactions between particular scenes produce predictable evidence. Only 12 combinations create evidence from the five scene types and the six evidence types including information, photographs, artifacts, biological material, fingerprints, and pattern marks. Each scene interaction has the modifying influences of the energy of the interaction, and duration of time interacting.

The evidence resulting from the interactions comes in high probability evidence, and low probability evidence. The challenge with evidence probability lies with the uniqueness of each scene. Any given scene and combination has the potential to produce evidence, even the low probability evidence. Some evidence can only come from certain sources, such as only humans produce fingerprints.

1. Person Scene and Person Scene:

a. Person scene high probability evidence: information, citizen photographs, trace artifacts, biological material.

b. Person scene low probability evidence: fingerprints, pattern marks.

2. Person Scene and Tool Scene:

a. Person scene high probability evidence: information, pattern marks.

b. Person scene low probability evidence: trace artifacts.

c. Tool scene high probability evidence: information, photographs, biological material, fingerprints, pattern marks.

d. Tool scene low probability evidence: trace artifacts.

3. Person Scene and Car Scene:

a. Person scene high probability evidence: information, photographs, pattern marks.

b. Person scene low probability evidence: trace artifacts.

c. Car scene high probability evidence: information, photographs, object and trace artifacts, biological material, fingerprints.

d. Car scene low probability evidence: pattern marks.

4. Person Scene and Private Scene:

a. Person scene high probability evidence: information, pattern marks.

b. Person scene low probability evidence: object and trace artifacts.

c. Private scene high probability evidence: information, photographs, object and trace artifacts, biological material, fingerprints, pattern marks.

d. Private scene low probability evidence: not applicable.

5. Person Scene and Public Scene:

a. Person scene high probability evidence: information, photographs.

b. Person scene low probability evidence: object and trace artifacts, pattern marks.

c. Public scene high probability evidence: information, photographs, object and trace artifacts, biological material, fingerprints, pattern marks.

d. Public scene low probability evidence: not applicable.

6. Tool Scene and Tool Scene:

a. Tool scene high probability evidence: information, photographs, pattern marks.

b. Tool scene low probability evidence: trace artifacts.

7. Tool Scene and Car Scene:

a. Tool scene high probability evidence: information, photographs, trace artifacts.

b. Tool scene low probability evidence: pattern marks.

c. Car scene high probability evidence: information, photographs, trace artifacts, pattern marks.

d. Car scene low probability evidence: not applicable.

8. Tool Scene and Private Scene:

a. Tool scene high probability evidence: information, photographs.

b. Tool scene low probability evidence: trace artifacts, pattern marks.

c. Private scene high probability evidence: information, photographs, pattern marks.

d. Private scene low probability evidence: object and trace artifacts.

9. Tool Scene and Public Scene:

a. Tool scene high probability evidence: information, photographs.

b. Tool scene low probability evidence: trace artifacts, pattern marks.

c. Public scene high probability evidence: information, photographs, pattern marks.

d. Public scene low probability evidence: trace artifacts.

10. Car Scene and Car Scene:

a. Car scene high probability evidence: information, photographs, trace artifacts, pattern marks.

b. Car scene low probability evidence: object artifacts.

11. Car Scene and Private Scene:

a. Car scene high probability evidence: information, photographs, trace artifacts, pattern marks.

b. Car scene low probability evidence: object artifacts.

c. Private scene high probability evidence: information, photographs, trace artifacts, pattern marks.

d. Private scene low probability evidence: object artifacts.

12. Car Scene and Public Scene:

a. Car scene high probability evidence: information, photographs, trace artifacts, pattern marks.

b. Car scene low probability evidence: object artifacts.

c. Public scene high probability evidence: information, photographs, object artifacts, pattern marks.

d. Public scene low probability evidence: trace artifact.

Scenes also interact providing secondary transfers. A person's shoes hold mud from a public scene field and deposit it on a rug inside a private scene home. A home's interior has no direct interaction with a muddy field. Scientists call this secondary transfer, or cross contamination. It happens with DNA where a scene transfers a person's cells to a scene where the person had no direct contact. Using fingerprint dust before collecting DNA from the same surfaces introduces outside DNA to the case. Dust and brushes used in prior scenes pick up DNA samples and deposit them on new scenes. Some scenes interact with more than one scene, such as a person holding a tool damages a car. Understanding this logic helps an investigator use the interactions to prioritize the scenes.

Information and photographs can come from the scenes themselves such as with computer data, or a smartphone camera. This section considers any scene capable of providing information to collect about it and situations to photograph.

No prior interactions between scenes makes for strong direct evidence from the first meeting, but interactions with a history of prior contacts work as indirect evidence with other circumstances. The investigator addresses the historical interactions within the investigation.

B. Functions. The investigator assesses scenes early in the process to make solid decisions about how to investigate them. An investigator's assessment focuses on a scene's functions, its volatility toward evidence destruction, and how to isolate it. Knowing how the relationships work supports identifying the roles of a scene. Scenes have several different roles at different times in the case. Places have controllers, owners, and occupants. Cars have owners, occupants, and drivers, as well as connections with places it goes. Persons control scenes and use tools during processes of crime. Following these connections increases the scenes available for investigation. A suspect chooses to commit a crime in a specific place offering privacy, security, and all the amenities he needs to complete the crime. Multipurpose smart phones provide conspirators a communication device during a coordinated crime.

Scenes have mechanical and legal functions. The two may have overlap, but also may present independent fact sets, such as when a victim fights off an attacker causing significant injury to the suspect.

1. Mechanical functions. Scenes occupy roles with specific functions to make things happen.

a. Central scene. A scene with multiple scene connections where the action happened occupies a central role in the case.

b. Bridge scene. A scene forming a connection between the suspect and victim acts as a bridge scene. Sometimes multiple bridge scenes connect the suspect and victim in a case, acting as links in a chain to connect the suspect and the victim.

c. Hosting scene. A container scenes host other scenes and actions like a public place, private place, or car. Investigators respond to hosting scenes, even if the action centers on persons or things.

d. Transit scene. A pathway scene provides a corridor for the persons or other scenes travelled through.

e. Staging or Support Scene. A base scene where a person works out of, exclusive of the crime scene, such as an apartment a thief calls home or a storage locker to keep stolen items.

f. Outsider Scene. Some scenes do not belong in a situation and have no natural reasons for presence. The situation also makes the suspect the insider. A cellphone dropped by a suspect in a victim's home during a burglary assumes the role of an outsider scene. A kidnapped person in a suspect's car with no prior relationship also assumes the role of an outsider scene in the suspect's car scene.

g. Occupant Scene. Some scenes exist within other scenes, such as a person within a home, or phone within a car.

h. Extension Scene. Some scenes act on behalf of another scene. A person uses tools or a car as an extension scene to do perform a task.

i. Action, Subject, or Controlling Scene. Some scenes do the action, and manipulate the scenes around it as in the case of a tool.

j. Receiving Object, Subordinate, or Controlled Scene. Some scenes receive the action, and hold the evidence from it. The receiving scene serves as a hosting scene too, but sometimes the hosting scene imparts evidence onto a mobile scene such as a person.

k. Focus Scene. The best scene available to the investigator becomes the focus scene.

2. Legal Functions. Scenes occupy roles with specific functions relating to responsibility for crime.

a. Suspect or Suspect Associated Scene. A scene has enough evidence connected with it for an investigator to allege a person committed the crime. The suspect scene controls subordinate scenes. Most suspects leave the hosting scene if possible.

b. Victim or Victim Associated Scene. A scene takes the role of victim if it received the impact of the crime. The victim scene controls subordinate scenes. The victim who summons help does so for a reason, and results in a greater volume of information evidence from the person.

c. Uninvolved Scene. Some scenes have nothing to do with the crime, and nothing to offer to the investigation. The investigator looks at these scenes to ensure he does not surrender evidence.

d. Witness Scene. Some scenes have peripheral involvement in crimes. Witnesses provide information as they observed or know about scenes, evidence, or events. They have a tangential connection, but access to information or evidence connected with the case such as a person out of town during a crime at his neighbor's house who finds evidence in his backyard. Officers carry the title of witness in court as they share their information.

C. Structure. Every scene type has its own structure which dictates its evidence producing and carrying abilities. The investigator's scene search builds on or corrects basic assumptions about a scene's structure to understand how the scene works. Each scene has restrictions to entry, layers, interaction points, and carrying capacity.

1. Restrictions. The investigator also determines the restrictions to the scene as part of how it works. These barriers like walls, doors, windows, gloves, and password protected computers have boundaries. Outside scenes produce evidence when they overcome the restrictive barriers to enter in scene.

2. Layers. The investigator understands the layers within a crime scene making investigations more challenging. Scenes have exteriors, interiors, subsurface, and informational networks.

3. Interaction Points. Scenes concentrate evidence in few places. Scenes bear evidence at the interaction points where the scene interacted with another scene including controls, communication lines, or force transfer points, all of which the investigator learns how to recognize. Once the investigator recognizes the points of evidence creation, collection becomes much easier.

a. Transit Areas. Scenes have funnel areas where other scenes must contact to enter, leave, or move about the scene. Persons use doors as transit points, but also walk down hallways.

b. Center of Gravity. Every scene has a center of gravity where the evidence concentrates. The jewelry box in a burglary or genitals in a sexual assault case occupy the role of center of gravity.

c. Target Point. Scenes have definable target points such as the storage locations of items of value.

d. Control Point. Scenes have locations where a person or other scene controls the scene. A person scene's control point may involve his arm for pain compliance, or a light switch in a building.

e. Impact Point. Scenes receiving action have impact points, such as where a bullet hit at car, or fingerprints on a window sill.

f. Forced choice or funneling. Scenes have structures which force choices on persons in them and funnel occupants. Some scenes like cars have forced choices about which seat to occupy, or a hallway funnels a person when going from one area in a building to another.

4. Carrying Capacity. The investigator determines a scene's carrying capacity by understanding what evidence created by interactions a scene can hold for the investigator to find. Carrying capacity centers on what evidence remains on a scene for the investigator to find. It keys on the scene's propensity to hold and

preserve evidence (good for the case), and the potential for other matter to replace evidence from unrelated interactions thus diluting the evidence (bad for the case). Different materials and surfaces have different levels of carrying capacity, and many scenes have multiple varieties of materials and surfaces in their composition.

a. Size of Interaction Area. Larger interaction areas where scenes had direct contact provide more opportunity for evidence presence.

b. Material. Some materials like sticky tape carry evidence better than others like a concrete floor.

c. Topography. Scenes with cracks trap evidence.

5. Volatility. The investigator assesses both the internal and external volatility of the scene. This relates to the scene's vulnerability to alteration after the crime and before the investigator works on it. Volatility impacts the investigator's ability to find and process evidence.

a. Mobility. A scene has higher volatility with portability, making it harder for the investigator to find and work it.

b. Remoteness. A remote scene or one difficult to reach can have higher volatility when it cannot be secured.

c. Environmental Conditions. The weather and environmental conditions around a scene can make for a volatile scene.

d. Accessibility. A scene with easy access allows persons to enter and destroy evidence, increasing its volatility.

e. Time. The passage of time increases a scene's volatility by allowing a greater chance of a scene interacting with the investigated scene.

III. Scene Engagement

A. Scene Priority Decision. The investigator decides what scene to work, and how to work it by aiming at the goal of finding the best evidence to prove who did what. She makes this decision with incomplete information. The investigator considers how the scenes came into view, and what information came with them. The investigator uses centrality and proximity to choose what scene to investigate.

1. Centrality. The scene connecting many scenes has a greater chance of holding evidence from those interactions.

2. Proximity. The scene connecting the suspect to the victim has proximity to the key relationship and evidence exchange.

B. Scene Management. The investigator must manage scenes to investigate them. The investigator must manage his own body as a scene with the potential to contaminate the other scenes by wearing personal protective equipment (PPE) like a hat, disposable mask, gloves, booties, and sometimes a bunny suit. All of those are designed to protect the investigator from harmful elements in the scene, and avoid contaminating the scene. Managing a scene includes: isolation, legal search, and physical search.

1. Isolation. Upon estimating a scene's value to the investigation, the investigator secures the scene to prevent the loss or tainting of evidence. The investigator creates a barrier protecting the scene as applicable for the scene types. Isolation reduces a scene's volatility, but cannot prevent destruction or alteration of evidence.

a. Control Access. Post a sentry ensuring no one accesses the crime scene without authorization, and inclusion on a record like a crime scene log.

b. Protect the Scene. If weather, sprinklers, or other environmental conditions threaten the evidence, canopies provide some cover. Floorless tents also provide side protection when wind threatens the scene.

c. Control Movement. Prevent the mobile scene from leaving.

2. Legal Search. The investigator decides how to search the scene and obtain the evidence while adhering to the legal protections of persons outlined in the Fourth Amendment of the US Constitution. The standards limit the government's ability to search and seize persons and their property. The court system treats evidence with the fruit of the poisoned tree philosophy, so unlawful actions result in losing evidence for court. The investigator includes why and how he searched scenes in the report.

a. Consent Searches. The owner or controller of a scene provides permission for the investigator to search. Some organizations provide forms for the consenter to sign.

b. Search Warrants. An investigator uses articulable facts to request a judge's permission to search a specific location for specific evidence which he believes located at the location.

c. Exigency. When the situation evolves and a delay could result in the harm to someone or the destruction of evidence the investigator may have no time to obtain a warrant so the investigator takes action to seize the scene to protect persons or evidence.

d. Safety Searches. Officers conduct safety searches with the goal of reducing the danger to officer and citizen safety. They pat down a person, look into objects, or enter a dwelling.

e. Community Caretaking. Officers search a place or object which appears abandoned or with suspicious circumstances indicating a person need help. Officers enter a house with a car in the driveway, and mail stacking up to perform community caretaking. They look at the call history of a found phone to find the owner.

f. Searchable Probation or Parole. When an officer wants to search a person already in the justice system searchable probation and parole provides law enforcement permission to search the person and the possessions and areas under his or her control.

g. Search Incident to Arrest. Officers have the chance and duty to search an arrested person. Depending on the situation, the search includes the area within reach of the person taken into custody.

h. Inventory Search. When officers arrest a person or tow a car, they have the opportunity to look in the car. This helps avoid finding dead bodies in towed cars, or allegations a tow driver stole expensive jewelry. Inventories fall outside the realm of investigations, but the activity results in the officer looking through a defined location to determine the contents in it. Whatever the investigator finds he uses as evidence, but courts frown on investigators using inventories to circumvent the laws.

3. Physical Search. The investigator also decides how to search the scene in a thorough and efficient method. He also finds and obtains the evidence from the search in accordance with accepted practices to ensure the courts accept it. Sometimes large scenes require a survey before developing a plan to work them. Poor adherence to proper procedures results in losing the evidence. The investigator has options as to the search type.

a. Lane search. Large and open scenes call for lane searches when many personnel search. A row of investigators stand shoulder to shoulder and walk in parallel from one line to the end. This allows for finding evidence in a short time.

b. Grid search. A grid search allows searchers to examine large open scenes like lane searches only they search the same area again by approaching from a 90 degree angle, so no person searches the same lane twice. This takes longer than lane searches, but doubles the searching and from different people and perspectives.

c. Spiral search. A spiral search works for large area scenes with few searchers available. An investigator winds his way outward from a point. This works well with a known center of gravity, or indication of significant locations, such as a piece of evidence.

d. Zone search. A zone search works well with natural divisions in the scene, or an investigator designates them. Zone searches address large or small scenes with flexibility to allow for fewer searchers, or accommodate more. Zone searches also make each person responsible for an area and allow an investigator to prioritize particular areas.

C. Evidence Plan. The investigator considers how the scene works, and how the evidence works to plan how to obtain evidence from the scene. The end of each section about a particular scene transitions from emphasizing scenes to proof through evidence. The order of evidence reflects a process of increasing from non-impact to high impact procedures. The information and photographic procedures continue to the end of the process.

1. Information anchors a case, and also represents other evidence. Information includes observations, statements, measurements, and historical information.

a. Observations.

b. Statements.

c. Measurements.

d. History.

2. Photographs document scenes and the evidence to show detail and context. Photographs include investigator photographs and citizen photographs.

a. Investigator.

b. Citizens.

3. Artifacts show ownership and control as part of physical evidence. Artifacts include objects, and trace.

a. Objects.

b. Trace.

4. Biological material proves identification of a lifeform. Biological material includes serology and DNA.

a. Serology.

b. DNA.

5. Fingerprints prove identification of a person. Fingerprints include latent, patent, and plastic fingerprints.

a. Latent.

b. Patent.

c. Plastic.

6. Pattern marks prove identification of a scene. Patterns include visual physical, chemical, and information patterns.

a. Visual Physical.

b. Chemical.

c. Information.

2.1 WORKING PUBLIC SCENES

Public scenes contain all other scenes and serve as hosting scenes open to the public, surrounded by loose, informal, or porous borders without access control. Public scenes include woodlands, fields, parks, roads, and parking lots. A public scene inside a building like a store, school, theater, or stadium, can call for the investigator to approach the scene like a private scene having more interaction points.

Goal. The investigator seeks to prove how a public scene hosted a crime, and what evidence its holds.

I. Case to Scene

A. Presentation. Public scenes seem to belong to no one, but often host several sub scenes and action. An investigator can find the initial public scene assessment difficult with the wide range of possibilities offered.

1. Active. Public scenes with active responses have chaos built in, but often with many ways to flee and endanger evidence.

a. Response. Emergency responses with lights and sirens provide notification of police response to persons in public scenes.

b. Scene Options. Investigators often have immediate access to public scenes during an active response to a crime in a public hosting scene if they can secure the scene early. An active response provides the advantage of containing the subscenes like suspect and victim within the public hosting scene.

c. Evidence Considerations. The faster the investigator arrives, the more chances to find evidence at the scenes.

2. Fresh. Public scenes with fresh responses provide a time window for activity in the scene.

a. Response. If the crime occurred within a few minutes of the 911 call, investigators may arrive soon, depending on the priority of the call. Person crime calls have priority over property crimes.

b. Scene Options. Investigators gain access to public scenes during a fresh response after minutes or hours. Often the suspect flees the scene, and the victim remains. The victim subscene often remains in hosting scenes while the suspects often leave it.

c. Evidence Considerations. Unsecured public scenes may lose some evidence during a fresh response, but continuous occupation by a conscientious victim or witness can preserve much of it.

3. Delayed. Public scenes related to delayed notification can have long periods of time between the crime and an investigative response.

a. Response. Some cases present to the investigator at the police station and the investigator drives a normal speed to arrive at a remote location, long after the crime.

b. Scene Options. The scenes are stationary, so referrals and walk-ins present unsecured public scenes subjected to tainting over time. Investigators may find minimal subscenes available, often only connected with the victim, although suspect connected subscenes may linger in the hosting scene.

c. Evidence Considerations. Delayed public scene response can have long reporting delays with the potential for the destruction of all evidence. Public scenes related to referrals provide stale evidence, but they can show how the structure worked with the crime.

B. Investigator Initiation. Investigators in a public scene rely on statements of persons near the action to define the scene and identify the relevant evidence. Observations while driving up to the scene, and from inside it help determine the boundaries. The availability of observable information comes with the problem of information overload with so many things to see. Historical information can provide recent crime history, or may go back years.

1. Observations about the public scene can yield many details.

2. Statements provide the information to identify the public scene. The reporting party who placed the 911 call during the action, made a statement of sorts, including a timestamp. Experienced investigators double or triple their initial boundary estimates to provide a margin of error.

3. Measurements about the public scene help solidify scene boundaries, and determine evidence within.

4. Historical information mines the internet and public information to provide histories of public scenes. Police records also cover prior incidents at the location.

II. Scene Analysis

A. Physics. Stationary public scenes interact with other scenes by hosting them. They only interact with scenes capable of movement and action. The passive nature and lack of build-up of public scenes often means they receive more evidence than they give to other scenes. They impart evidence of artifacts, and patterns on other scenes, while receiving information, artifacts, biological evidence, fingerprints, and patterns.

B. Functions. Public scenes function as accessible space hosting scenes and temporarily controlled.

1. Mechanical Functions. Public scenes provide unique sites for crimes in the least developed scenes. Distant controllers, such as municipalities provide little scene regulation, focusing on providing access. The controllers keep them natural or engineer them such as a park, stadium, roadway, or a retail store. Public scenes serve as the center of gravity, object scenes, but also transit scenes. The public scene of a neighborhood also hosts private scenes, such as homes, and cars, as well as persons, and their tools. Public scenes function as scenes to get to other scenes, or as public meeting places in most crimes. Most public scenes host the action between both the suspect and victim (if a person) and their controlled scenes as they come together, whether in an open space, roadway, or store. Public scenes provide anonymity to other scenes they host, challenging the investigator to connect with a person scene given the distance between the person and his activities.

2. Legal Functions. Victims or suspects only control public scenes for a short time during the period of the crime event.

C. Structure. Public scenes have undefined structure, or limited structure designed for loose interaction with occupants.

1. Restrictions. Public scenes have little or no restrictions on them. They have no barriers such as walls or gates to open and interact with, and less defined or nonexistent borders. Outside nature public scenes have no natural containment and only one scene instead of a perimeter or barrier scene. Public scenes have large volumes of scenes present in them over time and evidence of a scene's presence within the unrestricted public scene proves little by itself

2. Layers. Public scenes often come in a single layer, lacking the multiple layers from development. Public scenes do provide access to the earth, and buried evidence presents a challenge of discovery and a barrier protecting the evidence.

3. Interaction Points. Public scenes come in many configurations with a variety of interaction points.

a. Walls and roofs create barriers for piercing.

b. Doorways or gates funnel persons through a smaller area, and incorporate controls like handles.

c. The ground and pathways have surfaces to take impressions.

d. Parking areas serve as staging places, and high population scenes for transition from cars to person scenes.

e. Facilities such as restrooms have touch surfaces like faucets, and drinking fountains.

f. Gathering areas such as picnic tables in parks, or cashier stands in stores attract persons.

g. Persons discard evidence artifacts throughout the scene to create interaction points.

4. Carrying Capacity. Public scenes have high potential carrying capacities with their open space and higher potential populations. While the scene retains evidence from specific interactions relevant to the crime, the scene also retains evidence of countless other interactions. Consider the volume of persons who park in a wildland area, and go hiking. Along with the volume of evidence the scene carries, some scene parts lack the ability to hold the evidence. The environment causes a massive amount of evidence to flow about the area. Exposure limits the scene's ability to carry some evidence.

a. Size of Interaction Area. Public scenes offer large areas of interaction, but they also offer large possibilities, making the large interaction area a small fraction of the space.

b. Material. Public scenes can have natural furnishings like grass which can hold evidence, but they can also have concrete with little to grip the evidence.

c. Topography. Public scenes have little regularity in their topography. Some scenes have features capable of trapping evidence, and others limit the chance of showing any interaction with scenes.

5. Volatility. Public scenes have high volatility from exposure to the volume of interactions the scene hosts, and the elements. Persons such as suspects, victims, and witnesses enter public scenes with their own set of scenes and little resistance. They also destroy, replace or obliterate evidence of previous interactions through their latest actions. The elements also pose a threat to outdoor public scenes.

III. Scene Investigation

A. Scene Priority Decision. The investigator chooses a public scene as the priority when it hosted the action, retains evidence, and has the greatest potential for proof when compared to the other available options.

1. Centrality. Public hosting scenes can have a hub role for evidence producing scene interactions.

2. Proximity. Public scenes often only host the connection between the suspect and victim, unless the public scene assumes the role of the victim.

B. Scene Management. Public scene management can require a dedicated person to secure the evidence.

1. Isolation. Investigators may find defining the public scene difficult, which makes securing the scene harder. The investigator estimates the scene and doubles or triples the size to accommodate errors. Crime scene tape provides notice of a scene restriction and sentries prevent intrusions into the crime scene. The investigator protects the scene from the elements such as rain.

2. Legal Search. Public scenes owned by governments, such as parks have no legal restrictions making open to everyone, including investigators. Some private property open to the public like retail stores have restrictions requiring the investigator obtain authorization. Some subscenes within public scenes have more legal restrictions.

3. Physical Search. Large public scenes indicate a lane search or grid search. A spiral search works well in a public scene used for a transit route if the investigator has a point to center the search from. Investigators use zone searches for public scenes with natural divisions, or impose their own divisions on them. Public scenes may require investigators perform a neighborhood canvass and walk the area attempting to locate persons and evidence.

C. Evidence Plan. Public scenes collect all manner of evidence from other scenes interacting with them, and within them.

1. Information.

a. Observations. The investigator gathers observations about defining the scene boundaries, and the important components within scenes having larger spaces.

b. Statements. The investigator interviews persons to learn more about the public scene, its subscenes, evidence, and dynamics.

c. Measurements. The investigator's precise measurements of the public scene help define it, and the spatial relationships of subscenes and evidence in it. Fewer solid boundaries require more reference points.

d. History. The investigator seeks information from databases and other historical sources to provide insights into the how it has been used before in crimes, and routine purposes.

2. Photographs.

a. Investigator. The investigator photographs public scenes to show how subscenes, evidence and dynamics fit into an accessible open space. Investigators do not know the extent of the crime scenes in the earliest phases of investigation and take a lot of public scene photographs including useless shots.

b. Citizens. Persons and infrastructure show the public scene as a hosting scene with persons within. Persons inside public scenes may take photographs before, during, or after a crime with smartphone. The investigator may obtain these witness images from the person, or find them online at a photo sharing site. Infrastructure in improved public scenes may have cameras in high places watching over parking lots, gathering spots, stadiums, or retail stores.

3. Artifacts.

a. Objects. Artifacts show ownership and control as part of physical evidence. Persons bring artifacts into public scenes as part of a temporary control of the space. In some cases the artifacts preceded the events, and an involved person used them in the course of the crime. Persons find tools at the scene, or furnish the scenes with their tools and artifacts to commit the crime. Victims also furnish the scenes with their artifacts. Persons also leave artifacts in scenes by choice or accident.

b. Trace. Public scenes bear trace evidence as the result of scenes interacting and deconstructing. Biological based material in public scenes provides the potential for identification.

4. Biological Material.

a. Serology. All persons spill biological material in a public scene with a minimum of time in it. Biological material in unimproved public scenes may not have obvious places to find biological material unless contextual clues indicate a location. The investigator has the challenge of finding relevant sample from a suspect or victim. Sometimes persons use public places to do unexpected activities best done in private, such as having sex, and leaving a condom there.

b. DNA. Improved public scenes accommodate high populations of persons interacting with them, like stadiums. Handles, railings, and faucets, hold DNA, but the investigator has challenges identifying suspect DNA within the scene.

5. Fingerprints.

a. Latent. Unimproved public scenes often lack barriers, controls, or smooth surfaces, and a person may have no need to touch surfaces while occupying those scenes. Improved scenes like stores or gathering places often have human made structures for a person to touch. Anonymous samples or blind samples they have no solid connection to a specific person. Persons who feel anonymous, lack discipline, or have no plans to commit crimes may not wear gloves in public scenes. These tactical errors provide the investigator opportunities to identify the person. A public scene's higher population of occupants and rate of volatility bring a higher risk of evidence destruction.

b. Patent. Public scenes bear few patent fingerprints, but a lack of clean up tools provides the opportunity for a person to make them.

c. Plastic. Public scenes have limited opportunities for plastic fingerprints as they often lack of soft materials capable of collecting the print.

6. Pattern Marks.

a. Visual Physical. Public scenes lacking a barrier to entry also lack a pattern mark of a tool used to force entry. The scenes may have softer ground to accept shoe or tire prints. Improved public scenes often have paved surfaces not well suited to collect patterns although paved public scenes like parking lots and roadways hold tire and skid marks. Public scene patterns mimic the patterns legitimate persons create and blend into the scene more making them harder to recognize.

b. Chemical. A public scene hosts many artifacts made of chemicals, but the investigator chooses if the formula for the artifacts has relevance to the case such as with paint formulas.

c. Information. Informational patterns relate to public scenes as technicians identify graffiti by the message and signature of the artist.

2.2 WORKING PRIVATE SCENES

Private scenes contain many other scenes as hosting scenes with access control. Private scenes include houses, apartments, offices, tents, or any hosting scene with a barrier to entry.

Goal. The investigator seeks to prove how a private scene hosted a crime, how restricted access contributed to the crime, and what evidence its holds.

I. Case to Scene

A. Presentation. Private scenes always have an owner with an interest in the scenes and what they host, making them the most common scene type an investigator responds to. Their presentation resembles a public scene with the differences of a barrier, a designed and built scene, and a controller of the space.

1. Active. Private scenes often indicate a person present inside a protected scene with an ongoing emergency. The barriers to entry may pose a challenge to the investigator, but may also provide the opportunity to detain involved persons.

a. Response. Like public scenes, private scenes with an active response may tip a suspect off, stopping a crime from going further or resulting in his fleeing the scene.

b. Scene Options. A fast response and a secure scene can contain the private scene, and subscenes like the suspect and victim along with their controlled subscenes.

c. Evidence Considerations. Fast responses to private and secure scenes can preserve much of the evidence in the scene.

2. Fresh. Private scene fresh responses often mean cold burglaries, with the suspect long gone, but can also include a pacified fight with suspects present when the investigator arrives.

a. Response. A case within a secure private scene allows the investigator to get there soon after the reporting party discovered the crime.

b. Scene Options. Fresh response private scenes often only consist of the victim's side subscenes, but could hold both the victim and suspect for cases like domestic violence. The investigator may respond to a suspect controlled private scene, where the victim connected subscenes have limited presence, but high importance to prove interactions.

c. Evidence Considerations. Private scenes and their subscenes, even if a delayed investigation, can provide reduced yet robust evidence.

3. Delayed. Private scene hosted crime reports from walk-ins or flag downs indicate the emergency ceased a long time before.

a. Response. A slow speed response, sometimes delayed by a low priority property crime only call can mean hours or days between the commission of a crime and an investigator on scene.

b. Scene Options. With a significant time delay the investigator may only find either suspect or victim connected subscenes at the scene. Reduced scene options means the investigator searches for the outsider scene.

c. Evidence Considerations. Private scene referrals lag days or weeks, but can still yield evidence from a protected private scene.

B. Investigator Initiation. Investigators find private scenes easy to define, but they still need assistance in determining relevant evidence among the occupying items in the private scenes. Investigators obtain information about private scenes from wide-ranging sources but they have to correlate the information to establish the scene.

1. Observations. The investigator observes the private scene from outside and sometimes inside in the initiation of the case. The barriers for private scenes reduce many of the observations an investigator could make from a distance.

2. Statements. The reporting person who placed the 911 call during the action, makes the first statement to define the dynamic and identify the scenes with a system based timestamp. Investigators capitalize on person's self interest in their property with private scenes. Private scenes have a contact person who provides significant help in a case as he or she wants to protect the property. Most owners organize details and track information about their property. Some private scene owners provide lists of potential suspects, and lists of persons to rule out of the suspect pool.

3. Measurements. The investigator's measurements help solidify scene boundaries, and determine evidence within. The investigator collects few measurements in this early phase.

4. Historical. Investigators seek precrime private scene information from the inter-

net, and by restricted access databases. Sometimes an investigator taps historical information to learn who controls a private scene for the purpose of ensuring a legal search.

II. Scene Analysis

A. Physics. Stationary private scenes interact with other scenes by hosting them, while existing within larger public scenes. Private scenes only interact with scenes capable of movement and action. They impart evidence of information, artifacts, and patterns on other scenes, while receiving information, artifacts, biological evidence, fingerprints, and patterns. Private scene physics have two distinct areas and styles of the barrier to entry, and the center of gravity. Barrier scene physics center on a spot where a suspect used tools to interact with the private to scene to gain entry, although some persons enter via open doorways without contact. The interior scene physics cover the center of gravity in defined areas where persons interact with scene parts.

B. Functions. Private scenes contain other scenes like the public scene, but also fit into public scenes.

1. Mechanical Functions. Someone organizes the smaller space and designed structures with built-in subscenes for private scenes making them different from a public scene. Private scenes function as restrictive hosting scenes, protecting contents, and concealing activity. Most private scenes host the action between both the suspect's controlled scenes and a victim's controlled scenes. Private scenes may function as centers of gravity scenes in crimes, or act as support scenes for persons involved in crimes such as logistics bases.

2. Legal Functions. Sometimes the victim, suspect, witness, or other controls the scene.

C. Structure. Private scenes have defined structure from their design purpose to protect the contents.

1. Restrictions. Private scenes have a restriction to entry or exit creating a subscene where an outsider breeches the barrier. Sometimes the presence of a person or other scene within the private scene constitutes a crime on its own. When an outsider scene has presence in a secured hosting scene and the controller of the scene or the outsider does not authorize it, one person acts as suspect for false imprisonment, kidnapping, or possession of stolen property. Sometimes a person who controls a space provides other persons permission for presence, and one of whom commits a crime against another. Both suspect and victim take on an outsider role with permission and without breeching the barrier. A damaged private scene barrier indicates unauthorized passage through it. A lack of damage indicates an authorized entry, such as by key, but lock quality and human error contribute to questions about how a person pieced the barrier.

2. Layers. Private scenes have at least two of more lave including the exterior, the perimeter or barrier securing the interior, the interior, and whatever layers make up the interior such as furniture, and higher security areas like safes and hiding spots.

Private scenes have extensive background information providing a layer of history.

3. Interaction Points. Private scenes have at least two areas of interaction points: the entry point, and the center of gravity. Private scenes come with additional standardized interaction points.

a. Walls and roofs form barriers for piercing.

b. Doors, vents and windows with glass, handles, or sills provide points of entry and funnel points.

c. Environmental controls like light switches or climate control gain suspect attention.

d. Facilities such as restrooms have touch surfaces like faucets, and drinking fountains.

e. Places holding the items of value, such as a safe or jewelry box serve as targets.

f. Transit scenes like hallways between the two subscenes funnel persons in the scene.

g. Persons discard evidence artifacts throughout the scene to create interaction points.

4. Carrying Capacity. Private scenes have higher carrying capacities with their structured spaces. Persons design and build private scenes to protect themselves and their belongings. The protections also safeguard evidence.

a. Size of Interaction Area. Private scenes come with specific framework, contributing to defined interaction points which can reduce the size of the interaction areas. A suspect may only need to interact with a small area of a lock to break the door.

b. Material. Private scenes have human made materials contributing to carrying capacity. Humans build private scenes for comfort and safety, including hard smooth surfaces like windows, and doors, along with soft surfaces like carpet and upholstery.

c. Topography. Private scenes have all the variations of public scenes with uneven surfaces to collect evidence.

5. Volatility. Private scenes have lower volatility if the persons in control protect them to avoid contamination and alteration. Some scene wreckers have good intentions when they clean up. Suspects know enough to get rid of evidence. When a controller secures private scenes, the investigator has the option to delay processing those scenes to work on more volatile scenes.

III. Scene Investigation

A. Scene Priority Decision. The investigator considers the private scene for its centrality and proximity similar to a public scene as they both host. Private scenes offer high evidence potential.

1. Centrality. Private scenes host action, retain evidence. The investigator has two priorities in private scenes the barrier to entry, and the center of gravity. As a hosting scene, the private scene often occupies a central role in the case where the suspect and victim scenes interacted.

2. Proximity. The private scene can provide an intimate hosting scene for the investigation becoming the most proximate scene when the suspect and victim scenes present poor evidence.

B. Scene Management. The investigator finds the private scene easy to manage given most private scenes come with preexisting security measures.

1. Isolation. An investigator finds isolating a private scene easy when the structures of private scenes provide barriers and define locations. They also have roofs for protection from the elements.

2. Legal Search. The investigator needs the owner's permission, an exigence, or search warrant to search a private scene. If the victim controls the private scene, he complies, while suspects require the investigator obtain authorization by a judge. The investigator decides the appropriate way to search the scene within the law.

3. Physical Search. Most persons construct private scenes in zones, simplifying the search of pre subdivided the scenes. The other techniques work for specific applications such as looking for a special piece of evidence. Preliminary walk-throughs make efficient use of the investigator's time to coordinate the work for multiple zones.

C. Evidence Plan. The private scene evidence plan parallels the public scene plan, but requires the investigator pay more attention to the rights of the person or organization owning or controlling the scene. Private scenes also have barriers to entry as subscenes.

1. Information.

a. Observations. The investigator needs access to develop detailed observations about the interior of the private scene, but can make many observations on the approach to the scene.

b. Statements. The investigator can clarify evidence with statements from property owners or occupiers.

c. Measurements. The detailed measurements of private scenes offer the investigator insight into how the scene's structure influences the actions of occupying scenes.

d. History. The investigator has time to gather more detailed information about the private scene, and cross reference it with information collected on sight and from interviews. Someone owns or controls a private scene providing a paper trail on business affairs.

2. Photographs.

a. Investigator. The investigator takes photographs of public scenes using techniques to show scene dimensions, subscenes, evidence, and outcomes.

b. Citizens. Private scenes may have precrime photographs belonging to persons who have spent time in the scene, or in the private information arena, such as on some real estate websites. Sometimes they provide interior photographs of the home for a sale in the past. The occupants or their associates have posted photographs of the scene online or kept them. Private scenes may have cameras watching over the outside, entry points, transit scenes, and the center of gravity. Some private scenes have hidden cameras. Surveillance equipment keeps an eye on private scenes to provide footage of the event, or at least a pinpoint time. These phots lack complete coverage.

3. Artifacts.

a. Objects. Private scene artifacts show control, indicating an outsider or an insider. In some cases the artifacts preceded the events, and an involved person used them in the course of the crime. Persons find tools at the scene, or furnish the scenes with their tools and artifacts to commit the crime. Victims also furnish the scenes with their artifacts. Private scenes have far more artifacts than relevant artifacts. Victim, witness, or suspect guidance helps identify artifacts in the scene. The private scene restriction makes anything inside connected with a limited pool of persons.

b. Trace. Private scene trace comes from scene interaction to pierce a barrier, or interacting inside.

4. Biological Material.

a. Serology. A home or office hosting many guests has a smaller group of possible suspect biological evidence than a public park and offer better odds of a purer sample than from public scenes. Private scenes host, surround, and protect the evidence. If a person uses counterforensic methods like a hat to keep hair, gloves for secretions of oils, and a condom, he still discards DNA in the private scene in many ways.

b. DNA. Private scene DNA comes from interaction points with the ability to hold the sample such as the entry point, perhaps a light switch in a transit way, and the center of gravity. Persons in private scenes do all sorts of DNA connected activities, eat, sleep, lounge, fight, and have sex. One expects DNA from biological material such as semen in a home with adult males present.

5. Fingerprints.

a. Latent. Private scenes require a person travel through an entrance to the scene, interacting with scenes along the way. Private scene ownership means design for controlling the space more than for a public scene.

Many of the activities which provide DNA evidence do so without fingerprints. Persons have more likelihood to wear gloves in private scenes than in public scenes. Suspects controlling victims in their scenes do not force the victim to wear gloves, although they clean the scene of victim evidence. A secure area within the interior has a far more limited population of fingerprints than a living room. Fingerprints have more significance in the interior layers of a private scene, but fingerprints at the entry point also provide strong evidence.

b. Patent. Private scenes have the potential to provide a medium like paint, or blood for a person to create a patent fingerprint.

c. Plastic. The private scene also has the potential to host soft materials like unhardened putty.

6. Pattern Marks.

a. Visual Physical. Persons sometimes use tools to force entry into private scenes, leaving visual and physical marks. Private scenes host the same shoe and tire prints as public scenes.

b. Chemical. Many persons store chemicals such as cleaners in their homes or businesses.

c. Information. Some controllers of private spaces use informational patterns such as codes to unlock entry doors. Delivered mail with a person's name and address provide an information pattern indicating the person has a connection with the private scene.

2.3 WORKING CAR SCENES

Car scenes act as private mobile access controlled hosting scenes containing other scenes. Car scenes include sedans or passenger cars, roadsters, pickups, trucks, vans as well as motorcycles and bikes.

Goal. The investigator seeks to prove how a car scene hosted a crime, interacted within public hosting scenes, how restricted access contributed to the crime, and what evidence its holds.

I. Case to Scene

A. Presentation. Car scenes are a common scene type an investigator responds to as part of vehicular collisions and violations as well as hosting scenes. They have the barrier of a private scene, and can move within larger hosting scenes, while persons may also use them as tools.

1. Active. An active response to a car scene may mean an ongoing crime inside the car, with the car, or in response to an accident.

a. Response. Lights and sirens notify the public of a police response from a distance and could encourage a driver to flee the car scene if she has the capability.

b. Scene Options. Controllers of car scenes may not have the opportunity to remove the car scenes prior to the investigator's arrival to the hosting scene during an active response. Investigators may also have the chance to connect persons with a car when they are inside it.

c. Evidence Considerations. As cars make up the most mobile scenes, a fast response increases the odds of securing the scene, and by extension obtaining the evidence from a car scene both interior and exterior.

2. Fresh. The investigator must rely on the persons connected with the car scene either not knowing of a response, his sense of responsibility to stay, or a disabled vehicle, for the car scene to remain in the hosting scene before he arrives. Finding relevant cars challenges the investigator when persons remove them from the immediate and securable area before the investigation. Late report hit and runs means at least one of the cars left the hosting scenes.

a. Response. A timely response to a disabled car scene can yield as much evidence as an active response.

b. Scene Options. If the car remains at the location, the investigator may have all the subscenes in one place, with persons and their things inside the car. In minor collisions car owners often move their cars off the roadway for safety reasons, eliminating some scene parts.

c. Evidence Considerations. Timely responses to car scenes preserve the evidence allowing no time for its destruction.

3. Delayed. Victims have an interest in helping the investigator and victim controlled car scenes often help secure the evidence. Suspects also act in their own interests by moving their controlled car scene.

a. Response. Delayed responses to car scenes provide opportunities for the car, and the subscenes within the car to leave the area.

b. Scene Options. A car scene with time for the controller to act reduces the scene options for the investigator. A who arrives to a scene by a particular gar may not leave by the same car. Like with private scenes, the investigator may have trouble finding outsider subscenes on or in the car scene after elapsed time.

c. Evidence Considerations. Delayed responses to car scenes can reduce evidence on the exterior of the car. A person can clean both the interior and exterior in the time before the investigator looks as the car. Car scenes from referrals follow the same lines as walk-ins as the scenes have stale evidence and preservation relates to who controlled the scene.

B. Investigator Initiation. Investigators find car scenes easy to define, but still interview persons out of need for assistance in determining relevant evidence. An investigator can obtain a car's history early.

1. Observations. The investigator's observations come as he drives up, but the car's exterior shields the interior from his observation. Investigators observe the cars they can access. Observations include an account of where and how the investigator located the vehicle, and its condition. They attribute a controller if possible, and describe the appearance and condition. They also record unique features such as damage and personalization as way to identify the car among other similar cars.

2. Statements. As early as possible the investigator needs to interview persons to determine if and how a car had a role in the case, and who controlled it. A 911 call provides significant real time information. Callers find it easier to describe a

suspect breaking in to a car while watching him than describing him by memory half an hour later. Victims cooperate about the car scene under their control if it does not inconvenience them or they feel it benefits them. Information about how a suspect used the car in the crime helps the investigator locate significant evidence relevant to the crime.

3. Measurements. The investigator records measurements of the car, but often delays taking measurements until after determining the related information. Investigators often paint the locations of the car on surfaces to later measure distances include the car's specific location.

4. Historical. Each car has a permanent 17 digit Vehicle Identification Number. The number remains the same, regardless of license plate changes. Registered owners or short term possessors store information in the form of what they have done with the car, what they keep in it, and how they do it. Companies manufacture cars with specifications, identifiable by year, model, and color. The state DMV issues the license plates, and keeps registration records and histories of the car and owner. The local police jurisdiction keeps information about their interactions with the car and driver. Criminal justice computers also provide some of the same information, but also information the car's connection to crime. They also point to other agencies holding reports containing a connection with the car.

II. Scene Analysis

A. Physics. Mobile car scenes interact with stationary scenes by moving within public and private scenes, while hosting or interacting with mobile scenes of cars, tools, artifacts, and persons. They impart evidence of information, artifacts, and patterns on other scenes, while receiving information, artifacts, biological evidence, fingerprints, and patterns. Car scene physics have an exterior and interior. Exterior or barrier scene physics center on how the exterior of the car comes into contact with other scenes. Interior scene physics cover defined areas where persons, tools, and artifacts interact with the car scene.

B. Functions. Investigators find car scenes easy to assess for the same reasons as the high definition in private scenes.

1. Mechanical Functions. Car scenes function as restricted and protective space hosting scenes, and as tools under a person's control. Cars serve as hybrid scenes acting as hosts and tools. Persons use cars for meetings, offices, protection, or places for romance. They also use them for tools to store, and transport, and as weapons. Cars within a public or private scene aid mobility or serve as the center of action. Cars also act as the subject scene when a person uses the car as a tool or extension of his person to achieve an action. Mass produced car scenes with uniform features serve as hosting scenes, containers, tools, and objects of value. Car scenes have many similarities across the type, with many of the same controls, and features. Cars act as the center of gravity for a case, or a support scene to transport. The car's involvement in the case connects the owner and controller to the case, as the car person decides how to use the car.

2. Legal Functions. Most car scenes host the action between both the suspect and victim as they come together, or one of them, along with tools. Victim controlled cars host suspect evidence as an outsider, while suspect controlled cars may have limited victim evidence, but relate to a tools for the suspect's activities.

C. Structure. Car scenes have defined structure from their design purpose to protect the contents, and move them.

1. Restrictions. Manufacturers build car scenes to restrict access to and protect their interiors and trunks. Cars have barriers to entry like private scenes, but operate in high-visibility public scenes, such as roadways. They have interiors and exteriors. However, windows make the passenger compartment visible and sometimes accessible to outsiders, including seeing the driver. Persons have access to look in or enter into car scenes. Persons identify cars by their appearance relating to make, model, and color. Cars also have a license plate at least on back, and sometimes in front, as well as the VIN (Vehicle Identification Number, like a serial number) visible in the lower corner of the front window. Those two identifiers provide a key to access stored information in databases. VINs remain the same for the life of a car, while state DMV's issue license plates with registration.

2. Layers. Cars have several layers like private scenes. They have an exterior, a barrier, an interior, mechanical workings, and now data systems. Cars have a layer of background information stored by public agencies and private organizations. Each layer stores evidence.

3. Interaction Points. Car scenes have predictable interaction points based on control points, forced choices.

a. Car exteriors provide a protective barrier around the contents made up of plastic, metal, and glass.

b. The handles controlling access require touch to open the doors.

c. The tires interact with the ground to leave tracks and gather material.

d. Car interiors interact with persons and articles inside.

e. The driver's seat controls include the ignition, steering wheel, shift, rear view mirror, door, window, and seat adjustments.

f. Seats have cushions and function as a defined place to hold a person or artifacts and carry evidence associated with a specific event on them, such as sexual intercourse.

g. All seats have seatbelts, windows and door handles control the barriers.

h. Headrests have the potential to interact with persons' hair.

i. The controllable infotainment system provides information to the occupants.

j. Trunks store items for transport providing an interaction area including the locks to access the trunk,

k. Persons discard evidence artifacts throughout the scene to create interaction points.

4. Carrying Capacity. Manufacturers design car interiors for high carrying capacity for their interiors, including intentional storage spaces, and materials which collect evidence. Persons personalize their cars by the artifacts they bring into them. Artifacts provide evidence for identification of persons and actions. Companies produce cars to have limited carrying capacity on their exterior with an eye toward a sleek appearance and low drag. Cars cost time and money to fix their problems like body damage, which presents a carrying capacity.

a. Size of Interaction Area. Car scenes have easy to locate interaction areas. The tires interact with the roadway, and persons sit inside the car, controlling components. The interaction areas vary in size, but come with high predictability.

b. Material. Car scenes have a mix of human made materials providing various carrying capacities.

c. Topography. Car components have variations able to trap evidence such as carpet, or protected smooth surfaces.

5. Volatility. Car scenes have high volatility with their mobility, small size, and controllability by persons. Car scene interiors have high resilience. They have a combination of hardness and textures inside making for mixed volatility. Some evidence gets replaced by subsequent interactions and cleaning. Car scene exteriors have hard surfaces and textures with exposure to the elements and winds from driving contributing to .higher volatility. A person contributes to the high volatility by driving a car from a crime, cleaning it, or performing body work on it. Some suspects capitalize on a car's volatility by burning it.

III. Scene Investigation

A. Scene Priority Decision. Car scenes can have center or peripheral roles in cases which the investigator considers when deciding about working them.

1. Centrality. The investigator chooses a car scene as the priority when it hosted the action and retained evidence. The investigator may have multiple priorities in car scenes: the barrier to entry, the occupants, or how it fit within other scenes.

2. Proximity. The investigator finds car scenes as the main scene or as tools used to achieve a goal. Someone, suspect or victim, owns or controls the car, determining the proximity of the car to the involved parties.

B. Scene Management. The investigator can manage car scenes with ease as they are small, and movable.

1. Isolation. If an investigator can find a car scene, he can isolate it with ease by towing it to a secure location.

2. Legal Search. An investigator finds searching a car scene like a private scene, but with a few looser restrictions given the portability of the scenes. If the investi-

gator tows a car, an inventory provides the investigator an opportunity to look through the car's contents. In order to search them the investigator needs the owner's permission, an exigence, or search warrant. If the investigator tows the car, he inventories it prior to towing.

3. Physical Search. Car scenes tend to work best by zone, with the driver's area having high interaction, and moving through the rest of the passenger area, and the trunk. On occasion the investigator has reasons to search the engine compartment or examine the tires and their impressions.

C. Evidence Plan. Car scenes present easy to process hosting scenes with their size and limits on functions. Some collisions may require expertise with advanced training. The department may call out the Major Accident Investigation Team (MAIT) to handle the case.

1. Information.

a. Observations. The investigator's exterior observation provides context about location and appearance. Access to the car's interior provides the investigator with more opportunities to observe details for the case. Observations continue throughout the investigation if the investigator identifies the car. Unidentified cars require indirect information efforts to gather more information.

b. Statements. Persons provide context about the car, and can cover the dynamics of the car. The investigator's greater access to the car scene often triggers additional questions which persons may answer in their statements.

c. Measurements. Most measurements for car scenes come after the investigator has gathered information to determine the needs for measurements. Car scene measurements center on the car's location related to other scenes, dimensions, and specific evidence points on or in the car.

d. History. When the investigator has time to research historical information about the car he can unearth many facts about connections with other scenes, persons, evidence, and dynamics. Insurance companies also keep information about the car and driver. Jurisdictions controlling toll roads and traffic cameras provide access to their searchable databases of Automatic License Plate Reader (ALPR). The equipment captures the license plate of a car with a date, time, and location before or after an event to provide background information

Newer cars include onboard computers also known as black boxes, as a subscene of the car. Those computers record data on the car's speed, engine speed, braking, position, seats occupied, etc. They always record while someone operates the car, saving the data before a crash. Those last seconds provide a trove of information for car collision types of investigation. Those systems advance all the time, and collect more data. The onboard computer also records events like timestamps of when a window broke. Some auto sales websites contain specific car histories such as prior collisions.

2. Photographs.

a. Investigator. Car photographs show the car within the greater scene, such as a public roadway, or a private garage.

The exterior shots show the appearance and unique features including evidence. Interior images show the inside features and conditions, indicating how the occupants modified the scene.

b. Citizens. Persons in hosting scenes may take photographs of the car scene before, during, or after the crime. Most car owners have precrime photographs of the car. Hosting scenes may have cameras watching over the roads, parking lots, or ATM's.

3. Artifacts.

a. Objects. Artifacts in car scenes result from persons using the car as a mobile home, office, or crime machine as well as for routine artifacts, and tools. Most persons do more than drive in their cars, and integrate non-driving activities into their time in them, such as eating, drinking, smoking, talking on the phone, and listening to the radio. All activities require the person to interact with other scenes, creating more evidence. Artifacts may not appear out of place given most car scenes contain large amounts of evidence.

b. Trace. Persons leave trace evidence like biological material in cars, but they also collect other evidence like shoe dirt, or produce broken glass. Cars protect trace evidence in crevices, ashtrays, and under seats.

4. Biological Material.

a. Serology. Biological evidence shows up in car scenes as persons control cars by hands and they occupy them with contact. Even the self-driving car still requires interaction between a person and the car. Serology answers questions about a person's activities in a car.

b. DNA. Answers questions about who interacted with the car. The more protected the layer where the DNA located, the smaller the population possibilities for donors. Interior car scene DNA comes from most of the potential interaction points, but promising locations have the texture to collect and hold the recent DNA without holding too much of it over time. A smooth gearshift collects biological material from a recent controller. It presents a more defining option than a plush headrest which collected hair, skin, and oils from everyone who ever sat in the seat.

5. Fingerprints.

a. Latent. Fingerprints prove identification of a person. Interior car scene fingerprints cluster near identifiable interaction points with hard and smooth textured surfaces. The inner layers fingerprints have more significance for evidence, as presence inside a car crime scene means more control, and access.

b. Patent. The same conditions creating patent prints with other scenes work in cars. Forcing entry can increase the chances of a person bleeding to provide a medium for patent prints.

c. Plastic. Cars come durable, making plastic prints rare, but cars also hold whatever a person puts in them, so a person may introduce softer material into the scene.

6. Pattern Marks.

a. Visual Physical. Pattern evidence comes from events like collisions, forced entry, or sometimes controlling force. Car exteriors have high potential for visual and physical patterns such as tires which leave their marks on other surfaces. Manufacturers design the body of a car to crumple during a crash, and it accepts patterns or damage correlating with the damage of another scene. Suspects mark barriers to entry such as doors and windows when using tools to gain access. The paint has a chemical formula for a pattern, as does the glass and plastics on a car. The seatbelt leaves a pattern on a person during the rapid deceleration of the car during a crash, while inertia keeps the body moving forward. The steering wheel or deploying airbag also marks a person.

b. Chemical. The investigator may find the need to analyze chemical patterns in a car. The chemical rich nature of cars can make this area complicated.

c. Information. Modern cars involved several information tools as components. A key uses a specific pattern to operate the lock and the car. The key fob for remote door locks transmits electronic information by signal in a pattern form to identify and control the car scene. A seat's position helps indicate a driver's approximate height by its distance from the pedals.

2.4 WORKING TOOL SCENES

Persons make or use tools to perform functions. Tool scenes come in four types:

2.4.1 Hand Tool Scenes

2.4.2 Gun Tool Scenes

2.4.3 Drug Tool Scenes

2.4.4 Information Tool Scenes

Goal. The investigator seeks to prove how a person used a tool scene to perform a function in a crime, how it interacted with scenes, and what evidence it holds.

2.4.1 WORKING HAND TOOL SCENES

Hand tool scenes act as simple extensions of persons used to change a scene by direct contact. Hand tool scenes include hammers, knives, screwdrivers, pry bars, along with rocks. Hand tools' simplicity means a person could improvise anything and use it as a tool, such as an alarm clock for a weapon.

Goal. The investigator seeks to prove how a person used a hand tool scene in a crime, how it interacted within hosting scenes, and what evidence its holds.

I. Case to Scene

A. Presentation. In most cases the investigator finds the hand tool scene presented as a subscene of greater hosting scenes including public scenes, private scenes, and car scenes. Persons also carry tool scenes with them. In rare cases a person will bring a hand tool to an investigator. Some investigators may encounter a hand tool delivered by another investigator.

1. Active. Responses to active crimes with hand tools assume a greater hosting scene in which the tool plays a part and a person in control of it.

a. Response. Investigators find hand tool scenes in the possession or proximity of persons who controlled them in a crime when they arrive during or right after a crime.

b. Scene Options. Hand tools host little, and often fall under the control of a person as one subscene within in a hosting scene. Their value as a subscene competes with other subscenes.

c. Evidence Considerations. Early intervention provides the investigators more chances of connecting the hand tools to persons.

2. Fresh. Finding tools challenges the investigator when persons remove them from the immediate and securable area before the investigation.

a. Response. A fresh response to a hosting scene often presents in the same ways as covered for hosting scenes.

b. Scene Options. Most fresh responses provide contact with the victim who can indicate abandoned hand tool scenes connected with suspects. Sometimes the investigator responds to a suspect controlled scene containing suspect controlled hand tools.

c. Evidence Considerations. A fresh response gives a good chance to preserve evidence even if unable to connect the evidence to a person by possession or proximity.

3. Delayed. Victims may bring their tool scenes in when contacting an investigator, while suspects have time to move their controlled scenes. Hand tool scenes from referrals follow the same lines as walk-ins as the scenes have stale evidence and preservation relates to who controlled the scene.

a. Response. A delayed response to a hand tool scene could come hours or weeks after a crime.

b. Scene Options. Activity like when persons move or clean hand tools in delayed responses before the investigator arrives reduces the hand tool scene's value. Persons may move the hand tool scenes from their original scenes.

c. Evidence Considerations. Hand tool evidence in delayed responses can still work out well for the case depending on the hardiness and damage to the evidence by environment, time, and persons.

B. Investigator Initiation. The investigator can often make basic determinations about tool scenes in the early parts of an investigation.

1. Observations. Investigators observe tool scenes within scenes controlled by individuals or entities like private scenes, but sometimes the investigator cannot observe the inner workings of the tool.

2. Statements. Investigators with hand tool scenes find an easy to define scene, but an interview helps to determine relevant evidence. A 911 caller might describe a tool he viewed a suspect use or focus on the action and involved persons. The details of tools require a closer view for specifics.

3. Measurements. Companies design hand tools to perform specific tasks and construct them with solid parts an investigator can measure and observe. Detailed measurements come later.

4. History. The investigator needs access to historical information to figure out who controls the scene for the purpose of ensuring a legal search.

II. Scene Analysis

A. Physics. Mobile hand tool scenes interact with other scenes by moving within hosts of public, private, and car scenes, while under the control of person. Hand tool scenes interact with scenes capable of movement and action as well as stationary scenes. They impart pattern evidence, with information, and occasional artifacts. They receive information if they have information capabilities, artifacts such as trace material, biological evidence, fingerprints, and patterns.

B. Functions. Hand tool scene analysis focuses on function more than form. An investigator finds hand tools simple to assess in function, volatility, and isolation.

1. Mechanical Functions. Hand tools function as extensions of person scenes to alter scenes in a physical way while in contact with both the object scene receiving the action, and the person scene controlling the tool. They deliver force from scene to scene by channeling it for the person in control of the tool. They break, shape, puncture, cut, and build other scenes. Persons also use hand tools as objects of value. A piece of jewelry also serves as a medium for exchange acting as a tool for commerce.

2. Legal Functions. Suspects or victims can control tools, however suspect often use tools a means to achieve their goals, making far more tool scenes connected with evidence under the suspect's control.

C. Structure. Hand tool scenes have simple structures modeled on their purpose.

1. Restrictions. Hand tools fall under the restriction of their hosting scene or the person controlling them.

2. Layers. Hand tools have only their surface layer.

3. Interaction Points. Hand tool scenes have the basic interaction points of control, action, and sometimes an exterior middle area.

4. Carrying Capacity. Hand tool scenes have limited carrying capacity with a few hardened interaction points. Their texture plays a large part in how well the scene carries the evidence also, and sometimes they have textured grips more conducive to collecting DNA than fingerprints.

a. Size of Interaction Area. Hand tools often have small interaction points: a handle or control point the size of a hand, and an action point where the tool interacts with another scene.

b. Material. Persons make hand tools more durable than the material they alter. Their hardness reduces how much of the other scenes they can hold onto.

c. Topography. Hand tools may have cracks and corners to collect and hold evidence.

5. Volatility. Hand tool scenes have volatility from their portability, and low replacement costs. If the investigator finds the tool he finds the hardened materials survive many impacts with low volatility.

III. Scene Investigation

A. Scene Priority Decision. The investigator looks at hand tool scenes as the priority when they form a link between suspect and victim.

1. Centrality. The hand tool scene can hold a central spot in a case when it connects several scenes together. Hand tools can interact with the all scenes while under a person's control, but the controller only uses them in scenes requiring their functions.

2. Proximity. The hand tool scene often acts as an extension of the suspect or victim scene and interacts with the other. Sometimes tools only interact with peripheral scenes and they have low proximity.

B. Scene Management. The investigator can manage hand tool scenes with ease as they are small, and movable.

1. Isolation. The investigator can isolate hand tools by placing them in a box or other packaging to control access, their movement, and protect them.

2. Legal Search. A hand tool's legal search depends on the environment.

3. Physical Search. Hand tools require a zone search, for the action, and control subscenes.

C. Evidence Plan. Hand tool evidence plans focus on connecting the tool to scenes and what it can do, and the evidence shifts toward laboratory work.

1. Information.

a. Observations. The investigator may make additional observations of had tool under magnification or with the ALS.

b. Statements. Persons in the case may provide information about the use of the tool during the crime.

c. Measurements. Upon determining the hand tool's significance, its location measurements become significant also. Precise hand tool measurements may come in the lab along with measuring features on the tool.

d. History. Serialized hand tools have individual histories. The internet and reference books provide general histories about hand tools.

2. Photograph.

a. Investigator. The investigator photographs show the tool in context in a hosting scene. They also show identifying features, and a serial number.

b. Citizens. Photographs from citizens or infrastructure often show the hand tool in action, or associated with a hosting scene or person.

3. Artifacts.

a. Objects. Artifact may show ownership, control, and transfer of control. Hand tools may come with ancillary objects like carrying cases.

b. Trace. Hand tools pick up trace evidence from contact with environments. Crevices collect trace evidence.

4. Biological material proves identification of a lifeform. Biological material includes serology and DNA.

a. Serology. Hand tools have biological material all over, but often in highest density on the control points and action points if a person used the tool on another person. Serology can help show a person used the tool and the dynamics of interaction.

b. DNA. The investigator can identify who interacted with the tool by DNA.

5. Fingerprints.

a. Latent. Hand tools come with control points designed for hands which often hold latent prints well. Some materials such as foam or grip tape will not hold fingerprint evidence.

b. Patent. Greasy tools or tools bringing about a medium like blood or paint may create the right conditions for patent fingerprints.

c. Plastic. Hand tools rarely have soft materials to accept fingerprints.

6. Pattern Marks.

a. Visual Physical. Hand tools make good pattern marks. Someone designed them for greater resilience than the scenes they alter. Hardened steel hammer heads impact and mark the scenes they interact with, whether nails, wood, or persons. Clean up provides patterns also. A rag used to wipe away blood leaves swipe patterns on the harder surface such as a countertop or floor.

b. Chemical. The investigator may find chemical detection as useful with hand tools as with any other scene. Some persons use tools to work with material having a chemical formula for the investigator to identify involved entities.

c. Information. Basic hand tools rarely work with information patterns.

2.4.2 WORKING GUN TOOL SCENES

Gun tool scenes act as long reaching extensions of persons used to change a scene by force or fear. Gun tool scenes include rifles, pistols, shotguns, machine guns, muzzle loaders, and for the purpose of investigation BB guns.

Goal. The investigator seeks to prove how a person used a gun tool scene in a crime, how it interacted within hosting scenes, and what evidence its holds.

I. Case to Scene

A. Presentation. Person control and hosting scenes host gun tool scenes. They may also discard them in hosting scenes. Some persons carry guns with little regard for the laws, and no obvious relationship to the call. Given the severity of gun crime penalties and high replacement costs, persons often take them from their hosting scenes.

1. Active. Gun tool scenes present hazards with active responses. The investigator spends time and energy locating a firearm to both make the scene safe and obtain evidence.

a. Response. Active responses to gun tools come in the form of responding to hosting scene. Active gun tool scenes present the obvious safety concern for the investigator, as well as all the investigation concerns. The person controlling the gun may not want police contact increasing the investigator's difficulty by fighting or running.

b. Scene Options. Gun tools provide several connected scenes for the investigator to connect with a controller when fired. Even if the controller did not fire the gun, the investigator may find other controller related subscenes connecting a person to a hosting scene.

c. Evidence Considerations. Aside from the gun, the connected evidence can easily disappear in the chaos. An immediate and active response to a gun tool scene increases the investigator's odds of locating more evidence connected with the gun.

2. Fresh. Some gun tools remain in hosting scenes after crimes making them easy to recover in fresh cases.

a. Response. A fresh response may catch a controller of gun tool off guard and increase the odds of seizing it, however, suspect gun controllers often flee before investigators arrive to hosting scenes in a fresh response.

b. Scene Options. The fresh response scene options can differ little from active response other than safety issues.

c. Evidence Considerations. The gun tool evidence goes with the scenes. Time, the environment, and persons have time to alter the fresh gun tool scene.

3. Delayed. Persons rarely bring guns with them for delayed reports like walk-ins, flag-downs, or referrals.

a. Response. Delayed responses increase the safety with guns, but reduce options for investigators. Investigators may response to a suspect controlled hosting scene involving a gun tool scene.

b. Scene Options. The investigator may locate guns as the result of referral cases when the person in control of the gun either sees a need to have the gun, or sees no reason for concern about having a gun. Delayed responses to gun scenes may mean the controller has cleaned the gun after a crime, but before an investigator arrives and has secured it in its own subscene not connected with the crime, such as a gun safe. Someone may have removed the guns, but the investigator may find subscene components like shells.

c. Evidence Considerations. A secured hosting scene may preserve subscenes and their accompanying evidence. Chemical evidence from guns dissipates over time, but the pattern making ability remains stable.

B. Investigator Initiation. Investigators find gun tool scenes easy to define, but need ways to locate the gun along with the ancillary evidence.

1. Observations. Factory produced guns are as identifiable as cars with specific observable configurations. Many times the investigator only observes the outcomes of gun use. The firing of the gun and its impact happens in under a second.

2. Statements. A 911 caller might describe a gun he viewed a suspect use, but often lacks identifying specifics. In person statements provide more detailed information about a gun.

3. Measurements. The investigator often takes measurements after securing the gun.

4. Historical. Serialized gun tools have individual histories. Departments access records about specific guns while the investigator remains on scene.

II. Scene Analysis

A. Physics. Mobile gun tool scenes interact with other scenes by moving within public, private, and car scenes, as well as under the control of person. They project force on behalf of persons to victims and other scenes, so their proximity to other scenes varies for interactions. They impart evidence of information, artifacts, and patterns on other scenes, while receiving artifacts, biological evidence, fingerprints, and patterns. Sometimes the display of a gun gains compliance and alters the situation without contact interaction to produce evidence.

B. Functions. Gun tool scenes share features of compact tools with hand tools, but also have complex functions with higher volatility, and more challenges in isolation.

1. Mechanical Functions. Gun tools function as extensions of person scene to alter scenes in a physical way from a distance using force or fear. Examples of gun mechanisms include semiautomatic, breech load, bolt action, pump, revolver, and muzzle loader. Semi-automatic, bolt action, and pump guns eject shell casings while revolvers retain them in their rotating cylinders. Firing the gun makes the receiving scene of the bullet the center of gravity, while the person who fired the gun control it as an extension scene. Gun's accuracy diminishes with distance, but lack of accuracy does not make bullets less dangerous. Guns also have uses as objects of value like some other tools. When a person fires the gun, the bullet does the damage, but the gun connects to the person who fired it. Most firearms use cartridges made of a bullet, gun powder propellant, a primer, and a metal shell containing the parts. The process for firing a semi-automatic handgun involves a series of functions covered in the section on interaction points.

2. Legal Functions. Guns function as ways to force persons to control persons in crimes, and to cause damage or death. Guns serve as the central scene or an extension scene. A person can control the gun independent of who occupies the role of suspect or victim, and the investigator may determine the role of suspect or victim much later in the investigation.

C. Structure. Gun tool scenes have defined structure from their design purpose to deliver force at a distance.

1. Restrictions. Gun scenes have no restrictions.

2. Layers. A gun tool has an exterior and an interior workings layer. The bullet, casing, and magazine provide more layers for investigations.

3. Interaction Points. Guns have several interaction points like other tools, including the control and action points. Gun interaction points have connections to specific functions of the tool.

a. A gun has control points including the grips, trigger, stock, and sometimes a magazine or charging handle.

b. The controller aims the loaded gun which has a cartridge in its chamber.

c. Pulling the trigger activates the firing pin which strikes the primer, and the primer ignites the powder.

d. The burning powder creates a gas trapped behind the bullet, propelling the bullet out the barrel.

e. The gun ejects the remaining shell or retains it depending on the mechanism.

f. The bullet travels until it strikes a scene, and delivers the energy. Gravity, wind, and environmental conditions impact the bullet as it flies.

r bullet to target scene, and sometimes leaving a shell in a hosting scene.

4. Carrying Capacity. Gun tools have a limited number of carrying capacity areas. Guns have hardened surfaces with a variety of textures and crevices to collect evidence. Long guns have the same parts as handguns, but greater size providing more carrying capacity.

a. Size of Interaction Area. Guns have easy to define interaction areas of grips, which make up a good portion of the gun's structure. The size of the interaction area of the bullet can go unnoticed if the bullet strikes off target.

b. Material. Manufacturers make guns from metal, and other hard materials limiting their evidence carrying capacity.

c. Topography. Guns have textured grips, sharp corners, and crevices which trap evidence.

5. Volatility. Gun tools have high volatility from their direct connection to and control by person scenes, their high mobility, and sometimes concealability. A person wipes the surface of a gun clean. Holstering a gun or putting it in a case obliterates evidence. The resilient grooves and marking evidence from a gun remain identifiable after activity and link it to other crime scenes and the former controllers.

III. Scene Investigation

A. Scene Priority Decision. The investigator chooses a gun tool scene as the priority when it forms a link between suspect and victim.

1. Centrality. Gun scenes provide the controller an effective tool to control persons, acting as the central tool for crimes against persons. Most gun evidence connects a person to the gun, and the gun's bullet to an impacted scene.

2. Proximity. The gun scene can form a direct link chain from the suspect to the victim through the bullet.

B. Scene Management. The investigator can manage gun tool scenes with ease as they are small, and movable.

1. Isolation. The investigator isolates gun tools in a box to protect the evidence. Gun tools come with the caveat of unloading the firearm to prevent a negligent discharge.

2. Legal Search. Gun tools' depend on the environment for a legal search. The courts allow officers more latitude on legality of searches for guns as they fall under the public safety doctrine, but the narrowness of the exception excludes other evidence gained with it, so relying on the exception poses risks to the case.

3. Physical Search. Gun tools require a zone search for the different components.

C. Evidence Plan. The gun tool evidence plan shifts emphasis out of the field and into the laboratory. The investigator may interface with experts from a local crime lab for processing a firearm, or maybe the FBI. The Bureau of Alcohol Tobacco and Firearms may get involved with trafficking cases, but the FBI handles the more direct crimes.

1.Information.

a. Observations. The investigator's observations on location, control, condition, and identification of the weapon form the base of gun tool scene information.

b. Statements. Persons associated with the gun tool scene often share key information about the use of the gun, and other facts.

c. Measurements. The investigator takes locational measurements in the field of key positions like bullet strikes, ejected casings, and firing locations. Technicians take precise measurements such as used to compare casings in the laboratory.

d. History. Information about the gun, and who controls the scene helps the investigator to ensure a legal search. The massive market for guns and the robust investigative efforts have built a large body of information about gun tools. Precrime information about guns includes general specifications for the weapon, and what it looks like. Some guns have registration tying them to owners, or a documented history of involvement in crimes. Some databases have their identifying characteristics such as firing pin marks, and ballistics already on file. In progress information for guns comes from witnesses, and the predictable physics. Investigators obtain information about gun tool scenes as components of other scenes.

The internet and reference books provide general histories about gun tools. The investigator can query the internet for general histories about gun tools, or seek specific information from databases like The National Integrated Ballistics Information Network (NIBIN) or its component, the Integrated Ballistics Information Network, which stores gun information for the Department of Justice. Regional labs process guns and enter the ballistics data into NIBN. The searchable system enables pattern matching for bullets and shells, but also contains files on specific firearms. Other criminal justice databases provide searchable information about guns.

2. Photographs.

a. Investigator. Photographs document scenes and the evidence to show detail and context. The investigator takes photographs of gun tool scenes and the surrounding scenes. He also captures the serial number, model, and caliber to show the specific gun.

b. Citizens. Infrastructure and citizens may take photographs during the crime, but the investigator takes most of the shots. The investigator may obtain these images from the person, or find them online at a photo sharing site. Precrime photographs from NIBIN or gun catalogs help with information about the gun in a crime. In progress photographs come from the hosting scene.

3. Artifacts.

a. Objects. The act of firing the tool splits the gun tool into three object artifact parts: gun, shell casing, and projectile. The shell casings and bullets receive pattern marks after shooting.

b. Trace. Trace residue often called GSR comes from firing the gun and crevices collect trace evidence.

4. Biological Material.

a. Serology. The gun holds biological material on the outside and inside of the tool, providing a protected area to preserve the biological material. A gun's interaction points for using and holding it provide several spots good for collection: the grips, the barrel, the hammer, and the inner workings.

b. DNA. Gun based DNA comes in the form of sweat, but also other biological fluids like blood splashing back from a target, or in some cases saliva or vaginal fluid.

5. Fingerprints.

a. Latent. The gun's exterior layer carries fingerprints more than anyplace else. Like all scene surfaces, a fingerprint on a gun implies the last provable person to touch the tool. Two or three persons' prints on the tool provide a pool of potential controllers.

b. Patent. The investigator finds few patent prints on a gun unless in grease or blood.

c. Plastic. Plastic prints on guns have no way to happen unless someone applies a soft substance to the gun and then imprints skin ridge patterns in it.

6. Pattern Marks.

a. Visual Physical. The gun's firing pin marks the shell casing. The chamber marks the shell casing. The barrel marks the bullet. The bullet marks what it hits.

b. Chemical. Close firing of a gun causes the powder burns to mark the receiving scene. The burning gunpowder spreads around the areas where it vents from inside the tool marking the gun and surfaces near it.

c. Information. Guns do not provide information beyond the facts and do not provide patterns.

2.4.3 WORKING DRUG TOOL SCENES

Drug tool scenes act as a tool change a person scene by chemical reaction. Drugs include prescription drugs like insulin or antibiotics, marijuana, amphetamines, cocaine, opiates, and alcohol.

Goal. The investigator seeks to prove how a person used a drug tool scene in a crime, how it interacted within hosting scenes, and what evidence its holds.

I. Case to Scene

A. Presentation. Drug tool scenes come to an investigator's attention by their signs of presence or by impact on a person the investigator deals with. Drugs, like hand and gun tools, exist as subscenes within public, private, or car hosting scenes, or on a person. Persons hide drugs with ease. Some referrals and walk-ins seek out police while under the influence, but most do not possess drugs around police out of concern of discovery and arrest.

1. Active. Investigators discover drug tool scenes in the course of investigating a person or hosting scene. Sometimes the investigation centers on drugs, but other times the drugs are incidental to the original investigation like a fight.

a. Response. Active responses to drug scenes still provide suspects with opportunities and time to plan and execute a few moves to get rid of drugs, however many persons opt to retain drugs even when the choice places them in jeopardy.

b. Scene Options. Drug tool scenes exist within other scenes or under the control of other scenes and persons. Drug tools also come with subscenes like paraphernalia which the controller may find harder to separate from than the drugs.

c. Evidence Considerations. Active responses provide enough warning for persons to shed drugs, but other evidence relating to connected scenes provide a way to connect the tool to a person.

2. Fresh. Persons controlling drug scenes prevent them from involvement in fresh investigations out of self-protection. On occasion parents or unhappy partners summon the police and report on drugs.

a. Response. The compactness of drug tool scenes and options for a person to ditch the drugs provides little functional difference between an active response and a fresh response.

b. Scene Options. Fresh responses to drug tool scenes provide the same potential scene options as active responses Ditched drugs act as stand-alone scenes without their former controller possessor person scene.

c. Evidence Considerations. Drug tool evidence from a fresh response may provide good opportunities for biological material or fingerprints.

3. Delayed. Investigators conducting delayed responses to drug tool scenes go to hosting scenes.

a. Response. In many cases the drug tools are incidental to another purpose such as when an investigator looks into a domestic violence case, and finds drugs. Some persons bring drug scenes to the police for the same reasons as with fresh crime scene responses.

b. Scene Options. Drug tool scenes offer the same options with delayed responses as with immediate and fresh responses.

c. Evidence Considerations. Time provides controllers the chance to rid themselves of drug scenes, even though many possessor hold onto them. Stale drug tool evidence can still provide proof of control, and action.

B. Investigator Initiation. Investigators find drug tool scenes easy to define once found.

1. Statements. The investigator's interviews provide statements about the drug and its usage.

2. Observations and Measurements. Drugs come in measurable quantities with distinctive appearances. The investigator's observations center on close views, and indirect views of contextual indicators like paraphernalia and suspect activity.

3. Historical. Reference books and internet sites assist the investigator in drug identification and investigation.

II. Scene Analysis

A. Physics. Mobile drug tool scenes interact with other scenes by moving within public, private, and car scenes, as well as under the control of person. They impart more evidence of information, artifacts, and patterns on other scenes, while receiving less evidence including, artifacts, biological evidence, fingerprints, and patterns. Persons manufacture, transport, sell, or ingest the drug, and each activity involves different physics and assistive scenes.

B. Functions. Drugs function as tools to alter person scenes in a chemical and physical way when introduced to the person scene. Drug scenes have the direct function of causing a feeling in the user, and often a way to trade value for the supplier.

1. Mechanical Functions. Drugs originate in legitimate or illegal facilities where persons manufacture, synthesize, grow, produce and refine them. Some organic drugs like mushrooms and marijuana come with their own chemicals and the producer need only grow and harvest the plant in the right way for the chemicals. Chemists design drugs with specific formulas to produce desired outcomes, such as pain killing, hallucinations, or bacteria fighting. Illicit drug use revolves around recreation, addiction, poisoning, and controlling or disabling other persons, while legal drug use centers on curing a medical problem. Alcohol and now marijuana in some places represent recreational drugs.

2. Legal Functions. Most drugs function as tools to intoxicate and bring about a euphoric state of being. The standardized drug market ensures transportable drugs have standardized value and pricing. Drug possession makes a person a suspect. Drug use may make the person a suspect, or victim depending on authorization and knowledge of use.

C. Structure. Drug tool scenes have defined structure from their design purpose to deliver a chemical product to a person.

1. Restrictions. Drug tools come with restrictions defined by the hosting scene. The drug also has packaging to protect the chemicals. Drugs like pills or mushrooms require nothing more than the drug, but other drugs require paraphernalia or tools for administering the drug.

2. Layers. Drug tools have packaging separating the outside from the chemical composition. They also have a layer of information.

3. Interaction Points. Drugs come in several forms: pill, powder, liquid, gas, dissolved on paper or other material, and plant material. Drugs interact with persons or packaging and packaging interacts with its storage environment, and whoever touches it. The person consuming the drug interacts with it and shows the impact in various body functions

4. Carrying Capacity. Form and size provide drugs with limited carrying capacity to retain evidence from interaction with other scenes.

a. Size of Interaction Area. Drugs have small interaction areas, and most drugs are protected by packaging creating and intermediary for evidence collection.

b. Material. Drugs do not hold evidence well, but the plastic packaging may collect evidence.

c. Topography. Rough or smooth drug surfaces do not hold evidence well.

5. Volatility. Most drugs come in stable chemical compounds, although alcohol evaporates. Once a person introduces the chemicals into a body, they break down in order to alter the body. The body converts the chemicals and discards the waste.

III. Scene Investigation

A. Scene Priority Decision. The investigator chooses a drug tool scene as the priority when it represents the main component of a law violation. The investigator working with a drug tool has limited options for evidence centering on its chemical makeup.

1. Centrality. Drug tool scenes achieve an action, but have low ability to collect evidence.

2. Proximity. The drug scene does not often form a link between suspect and victim.

B. Scene Management. The investigator can manage drug tool scenes with ease as they are small, and movable.

1. Isolation. Investigators isolate drugs to ensure no cross contamination of the sample, and for safety as many drugs contain harmful substances.

2. Legal Search. Drug tools depend on their environment to determine the legal search method.

3. Physical Search. An investigator searches for drugs by recognizing the material, packaging, appearance, and smell. Texture provides another physical sensory clue. The investigator uses sensory perceptions as support to move forward with a presumptive test to identify the substance before sending it to a lab for definitive testing and identification.

C. Evidence Plan. The investigator's evidence plan centers on identifying an alleged drug, and connecting it with a person. This process moves from the field to the lab with the chemical tests required of the evidence.

1. Information.

a. Observations. The investigator's initial observations help him identify a substance as a probable drug. The investigator observes the hosting area, appearance, packaging, odors, and who controls what.

b. Statements. Sometimes statements can clarify the body of information about a suspected drug including control and ownership.

c. Measurements. Precise drug scene measurements like weight often come in the lab after recording a basic count of packages.

d. History. The drug field changes all the time with successive waves of invention, popularity, and laws. Drug laws vary by region. Many districts have decriminalized drugs. A drug's legality changes under certain circumstances, or prescription, use, quantity, and outcome. A lot of drug tool information comes from outside sources, including technical details for drug manufacturing, packaging, storing, use, and product reviews

2. Photographs.

a. Investigator. The investigator takes most photographs relating to drug scenes. The investigator documents the hosting scene, the controller, proximity to control by persons, the packaging, and drugs themselves.

b. Citizens. Sometimes citizens may take drug themed photographs during the crime as party shots. Persons may take photographs before, during, or after a crime showing the drug tool. The investigator obtains these images from the person or online at a photo sharing site. The investigator takes photographs of private scenes.

3. Artifacts.

a. Objects. Drugs come with artifacts of packaging and paraphernalia.

b. Trace. Drugs often have trace chemicals with them such as what dealers use to cut the drugs and expand their product.

4. Biological Material.

a. Serology. Drugs have the potential to hold biological material on the packaging, but multiple possessors spanning time and locations provide the investigator with samples from persons in other countries and continents complicates the process.

b. DNA. Drugs can hold DNA within biological material like with other evidence, but bears the same problems as with serology.

5. Fingerprints.

a. Latent. Drug scenes hold fingerprints on the packaging like a plastic bag. Drugs have a low chance of having fingerprints, but some connected scenes like paraphernalia or pill bottles act as interaction points to collect them.

b. Patent. If a drug scene has involvement with a medium to transfer the fingerprint it could bear a patent print, although unlikely.

c. Plastic. Drugs rarely have soft surfaces, but some like resinous marijuana or hash resemble putty.

6. Pattern Marks.

a. Visual Physical. Pharmaceutical pills have numbers stamped on them to provide identification information. Some illicit laboratories stamp their pills as a form of branding and marketing. Any drug dealer can use distinctive packaging such as bags with logos.

b. Chemical. The drug's chemical formula also dictates how it reacts with a person in order to bring about a change in the person scene. The chemical pattern distinguishes the crime of the drug assuming the absence of authorization for possession of the chemical.

c. Information. The information pattern stamped on pills can provide a way to search the drug.

2.4.4 WORKING INFORMATION TOOL SCENES

Information tool scenes act as extensions of persons used to process and transfer information. Information tools process information on behalf of a person and include private tools like smartphones, car black boxes, personal computers, or even pencil and paper as well as public tools like ATMs.

Goal. The investigator seeks to prove how a person used an information tool scene in a crime, how it interacted within hosting scenes, and what evidence its holds.

I. Case to Scene

A. Presentation. Information tool scenes come into investigations like the other tools as component subscenes within public, private, or car scenes, and often under the control of a person. The wide adoption of smartphones has provided almost every person scene with an attached information tool scene.

1. Active. Information tool scenes with active responses relate to the hosting scenes, and the person in control of the tool.

a. Response. An active response can seem fast for hand tools, but information tools work in microseconds, giving the controller time to act.

b. Scene Options. Information tools can act as the key subscenes among the choices of scenes to investigate. Most communication enabled information tools have subscenes of their own in the immediate area, but they also have the subscene of whatever they connect to such as an internet database also known as the cloud.

c. Evidence Considerations. Information tools in active crime scene responses often center on physical evidence in the initial part, with follow up for technical forensics to obtain the data.

2. Fresh. Information tool scenes associated with fresh crime scene responses offer modest potential as time allows an opportunity for the alteration or destruction of evidence.

a. Response. A fresh response to an information tool scene can still provide access to information tools.

b. Scene Options. Information tool scene options depend on access to the controller of the tools. Victim controlled information tools often provide more complete scene options, while suspect controlled information tools provide reduced scene options. The odds of working with a suspect controlled information tool go down with the passage of time.

c. Evidence Considerations. Like all tools, the accessibility of information tools dictates the evidence available to the investigator with fresh responses.

3. Delayed. The scene controller has great control over how much evidence portable information tools retain in walk-in reports. Reporting parties leave public information tools like ATMs unsecured when contacting the authorities.

a. Response. Delayed responses to information tools may still provide good investigative options to the investigator. Information tools associated with referrals may still retain evidence depending on settings and who controls the tool. However, referral responses like fresh responses give the investigator time to research the tool if enough initial information exists.

b. Scene Options. No matter how delayed the investigation, the information tool often has its internal memory as a scene available. The remotely connected information tool such as a mainframe computer or telephone system provides a long preserved information tool scene.

c. Evidence Considerations. Information tools provide evidence long after the crime, and a delayed response may still access the evidence, albeit from remote sources.

B. Investigator Initiation. Investigators with information tool scenes find an easy to define physical scene, but still need other ways to locate the evidence within its virtual sphere. Investigators obtain information about information tool scenes as components of other scenes.

1. Observations. The investigator may only observe the exterior of information tools, and miss the inner workings of the machine.

2. Statements. In person statements may provide no detailed information about information tool scenes. Person scenes control information tool scenes, and their statements help the investigator define parts of the case.

3. Measurements. Factories manufacture information tools with distinctive attrib-

utes. The internet provides diagrams of information tools, and the investigator can sketch them like any other tool.

4. Historical. Historical information may help determine who controls the scene for the purpose of ensuring a legal search. Internet sites assist the investigator in information tool investigation. Mass produced information tools have great amounts of information about them on the internet. Specialized groups such as banking and credit card anti-fraud units also provide information about the tools they see used with crime on a regular basis. Many scene types have built in information tools which provide information about what happened in or with the scene. Cars have black boxes, hosting scenes have security systems, many tools include computers, and people now monitor their bodies with computers connected with the internet.

II. Scene Analysis

A. Physics. Mobile information tool scenes can interact with scenes by moving within public, private, and car scenes. Stationary information tools interact with other scenes by electronic connection. Information tool scenes interact with scenes capable of movement and action as well as stationary scenes. They impart evidence of information and patterns on other scenes, while receiving information, artifacts, biological evidence, fingerprints, and patterns. Information tools have virtual and physical spheres of interactions. The tool has a two way flow of sending and collecting information, while the exterior of the tool collects evidence.

B. Functions. Personal information tools function as extensions of a person scene to process, and transfer information into a data form. Information becomes data or useful facts and details from the information.

1. Mechanical Functions. The physical tool contains the hardware and controlling software where the important action happens inside. Information tools contain information and action history from processing and transferring information. The tools process information as representations of the world coming from input devices including keyboards, sensors, and other tools. Some information tools like monitoring equipment connected with other scenes function as extensions of those scenes. The tool uses data to perform tasks for the controller, such as opening doors, transferring funds, or recording actions. Information tools process and transfer information on behalf of persons, whether suspect or victim, while within any of the five scene types, as well as in the virtual realm.

Information tools act as the center of gravity for some cases when they process, store, and transfer so much information about the crimes committed. Valuable and portable electronics also serve as a way to transfer value. Identity theft cases must have information tools for the suspect to use information to steal.

2. Legal Functions. Information tools link the suspect and the center of gravity as persons use information tools as a way to communicate in conspiratorial crimes,

such a robbery gangs. Persons also use information tools to steal by manipulating information.

C. Structure. Information tool scenes have defined structure from their design purpose to receive, process, and send information.

1. Restrictions. All information on an information tool has authorized, or unauthorized presence. Information tools have restrictions of the hosting scene like the rest of the tools. They have an unrestricted exterior to provide limited access. They also have a restricted interior where the tool safeguards information as a valuable subscene. Information tools require authentication when they interact with other information tools, making a significant barrier to entry for both outsiders and investigators. Access requires a technical expert to get to the data from within the tool.

2. Layers. Information tools have four layers. the exterior, the hardware, the software, and the network connection. The tools also have a layer of information from the manufacturer and public agencies if the tool has a history of interaction with crime.

3. Interaction Points. Electronic information tools have interaction zones for each of their layers, and each layer has different ways of interacting with other scenes in the physical and virtual worlds.

a. The exterior provides a surface to interact with the surrounding scenes, including a person controlling the tool.

b. The tool has hardware interactions, and software interactions such as wiring, broadband, wi-fi, a hotspot, or satellite uplink.

c. The tool also connects with other scenes to transfer data.

d. It obtains information from sensors, or input devices like keyboards.

4. Carrying Capacity. Information tools have limited physical carrying capacity for their physical scenes, but they have near limitless recording capacity of actions. The authentication process shows specific interactions with other scenes through recording identification information.

a. Size of Interaction Area. Information tools have moderate sized physical interaction areas to build evidence from controller interactions. The information interaction areas often exist in the virtual realm making them small, and requiring knowledge of where to look.

b. Material. Smooth glass and plastic surfaces of most information tools collect some evidence well.

c. Topography. Information tools have smooth surfaces to collect some evidence types well, such as fingerprints and biological materials, but the lack of crevices hinder the accumulation of other evidence like trace.

5. Volatility. The exterior of information tools carry the same volatility as any

hand tool. Information tools' portability and controllability allow a person to erase the history of actions.

III. Scene Investigation

A. Scene Priority Decision. The investigator chooses an information tool scene as the priority when it represents what the controller thought and did relating to a law violation. Some information scenes track persons' actions, locations, questions, and contacts. It can also form a link between suspect and victim.

1. Centrality. The information tool scene can occupy a central hub role in a case when it can show planning, thoughts, communications, and locations. Smartphones also have an increasing role in finances, which facilitate many crimes.

2. Proximity. The information tool scene may connect the suspect and victim controlled scenes, but often the tool has higher proximity to the suspect, unless the suspect took over the victim controlled tool.

B. Scene Management. The investigator can manage some information tool scenes with ease as they are small, and movable. Some scenes are large data systems requiring less controlling methods to gain access to the scene. Locked down data systems may cripple an organization's operation more than the actual crime.

1. Isolation An investigator isolates an information tool with each in the physical sense by boxing it up, but information tools using wireless communication require methods to block signals from controlling the machine or altering the data on it. Some agencies put smartphones in Faraday boxes to prevent them from connecting with anything and enabling remote control.

2. Legal Search. The legality of searching an information tool depends on the environment, but the Fourth Amendment protects information tools from searches without warrants. Most persons keep information tools under close control, such as on their person, in their car, or home. If someone separates the information tool from a restrictive scene, the investigator still decides how to search within the law.

3. Physical Search. Investigators search information tools by zone searches for their physical exterior and software interior. The investigator can expand the physical search of an information tool to off-site connections, such as a phone service billing, or internet connection which stores copies of their records.

The investigator counters high volatility by knowing the identification of the information tool like the International Mobile Equipment Identity number (IMEI), a 15 digit code identifying each cellphone or mobile broadband device, and what scenes the tool interacted with such as websites or an Internet Service Provider (ISP), a local area network (LAN) or wi-fi (wireless router for multiple devices to have communications with each other and the internet).

C. Evidence Plan. The investigator looks to prove physical control of an information scene while also proving a flow of information between the controller and either another person with a device, or a data system.

1. Information.

a. Observations. The investigator often collects limited observations about the information tool during and after the search. Observations of information tools can include equipment set ups, the displayed information, and deeply stored data. The investigator notes the device model and serial number, operating system, and who had control of the device, and proximity.

b. Statements. The investigator may collect some kind of statement about an information system, unless the suspect controls the tool. Under those circumstances a victim or witness may have a statement relating to the tool, or the functional outcome related to using a tool.

c. Measurements. Information tools require almost no measurements in a physical sense, and the tool presents the information in a measured way with timestamps, locations, and contacts. The investigator measures proximities to persons and other scenes.

d. History. The investigator working with an information tool has near unlimited options for evidence centering on data about what the controller did, where he went, and who he communicated with when searching the tool.

2. Photographs.

a. Investigator. The investigator takes photographs of information scenes Photographs document scenes and the evidence to show detail and context. The photographs show the information tool in context of its hosting scene. The images should also show a make, model, and serial number. If the tool has operating system software, photographs can capture the version, along with additional software.

b. Citizens. Some information scenes like phones, computers, and ATMs have cameras built into them, providing photographs from the infrastructure of the scene. Persons may take photographs before, during, or after a crime showing the information tool. The investigator obtains these images from the person, or finds them online at a photo sharing site.

3. Artifacts.

a. Objects. Most persons own multiple information tools, and interact with other public information tools. Some information tools come with ancillary scenes like cases, cables, and other information tools.

b. Trace. Information tools can have trace evidence connecting them to scenes such as dirt, and biological materials.

4. Biological Material.

a. Serology. Persons control information tools and the tools often require the controller to touch them. Most information tools have less emphasis on what part of the body, and more on whose body controlled the device.

b. DNA. Persons touch cellphones, and then hold them to their face when using them providing many opportunities for material transfer.

The interiors of private information such as battery compartments also provide protected sources. Public information tools provide blind samples, and the investigator often finds them too nonspecific for labs to sequence.

5. Fingerprints.

a. Latent. Information tools collect fingerprints their control points. Many information tools have glass and hard plastic surfaces. The battery compartment provides a cache of fingerprint evidence.

b. Patent. Unless the environment provides a liquid medium, patent prints are unlikely.

c. Plastic. Information tools lack soft materials to accept prints, and could only do so if added to the scene.

6. Pattern Marks.

a. Visual Physical. The information machine centers on the information world, but sometimes a person uses one as a tool outside its design intention, such as hitting another person in the face with a cellphone.

b. Chemical. Information tools rarely have use as carriers for chemical purposes, but it could trap trace chemicals.

c. Information. Information tool pattern evidence could form the same way as it would with any hand tool, but if a person uses the tool in the intended manner, information tools provide information pattern evidence. Passwords authenticate the tool to allow for actions. A handshake between information tools ensures an authorized interaction to establish the connection where the two trade information back and forth Information tools work with codes or patterned information. Many schools have their students submit their papers to a plagiarism engine to check patterns in writing to see if the writing matches already established work.

2.4.5 WORKING PERSON SCENES

Person scenes act as the origin scene for crimes by way of thoughts and actions. Suspects are always person scenes. Persons have roles of suspect, victim, and witness in a case. Person scenes include humans, and for the purposes of evidence collection animals.

Goal. The investigator seeks to prove what a person did in a crime, how he or she interacted within hosting scenes, and what evidence he or she holds.

I. Case to Scene

A. Presentation. Person scenes factor into every scene, either in front as controller, or in back as impacted. The person scene always exists within a hosting scene, even if not the crime scene. The person also controls subscenes.

1. Active. A person scene with an active response indicates involvement in crime activity, either as a suspect or victim.

a. Response. An emergency response can tip off persons in an active crime, and result in either the danger reducing, or intensifying.

b. Scene Options. Person scenes receiving an active response make up a subscene within a hosting scene interacting with other scenes to create evidence in the present or recent past. If the case involves direct combat between the suspect and victim, the majority of evidence revolves around the two, and their subordinate scenes.

c. Evidence Considerations. Person scenes lose evidence as soon as they produce it. An active crime scene response gives the investigator the best opportunity of obtaining the most evidence from the person scenes

2. Fresh. Delayed responses to person scenes provide the investigator with lower

likelihood of investigating all persons in a case, and the loss of evidence for the persons still available.

a. Response. A fresh response to a person scene looks similar to an active response, with more time in arriving.

b. Scene Options. More time means one of the scenes often flees prior to investigator arrival, reducing the investigator's available choices.

c. Evidence Considerations. The remaining scenes could have stale and damaged evidence, but a lot of evidence associated with person scenes has enough survivability to last a few hours or even days depending on the carrying person's activities.

3. Delayed. Person scenes who walk-in or flag down an officer to report a crime almost always do not have both suspect and victim present, meaning a significant part of the evidence remains outstanding.

a. Response. The investigator's delayed response to a person scene after days or weeks provides limited value in a case, but sometimes enough to move the case forward.

b. Scene Options. Delayed cases of referrals and walk-ins rely on a victim person scene, even if naming the suspect scene. Investigators may travel to see a suspect person scene after a delay, yet the person may still have connections to other subscenes.

c. Evidence Considerations. The time delay of a few days to weeks often erodes the physical evidence, and allows some evidence to change, such as bruising to heal. On the other end of the spectrum, some evidence remains unchanged with the passage of time.

B. Investigator Initiation. Investigators talk with persons to get the initial information, which equates to close interaction with scenes. Person scene information covers everything from general biology to a particular person's specific details including how a person scene looks, feels, and acts after an interaction. Depending on the type of crime and who the investigator speaks with, the person provides information for the investigator to corroborate or refute. The first person to approach the investigator tells a history of events from his perspective with a goal for the investigation and sees the investigator as the way to get it. Many persons who report crimes claim victimhood, but the investigator still must verify the claim by facts through evidence. Guiding a conversation toward evidence sets the investigation up for success. The investigator also observes persons for appearances, actions, and statements. The investigator also used historical information about the person as background for the crime.

1. Observations. Investigators interact with persons by observing from a distance and continues up close throughout contact. The investigator looks for signs of a struggle, or drug abuse signs and symptoms, or even discomfort and evasive answers to basic questions.

2. Statements. The 911 call provides an in progress recording of events as they happen instead of a recollection of the events. Humans have memory capability, but the brain filters and modify the memories to slant the presentation of memories. Initial statements about basic details set the tone for the investigation.

3. Measurements. The investigator holds off on measurements during the initial contact with a person until certain of their necessity.

4. Historical. Many times persons accumulate extensive searchable background information searchable via the internet, or criminal records of previous cases. If the person scene falls under control of another agency, then the report becomes historical information.

II. Scene Analysis

A. Physics. The person scene has the most complex features, and can create the most evidence as persons think, act, and react to the scenes around them. Mobile person scenes interact with other scenes by moving within public, private, and car scenes, as well as controlling cars, tools, and artifacts. Person scenes impart evidence of information, artifacts, biological evidence, fingerprints, and patterns on other scenes, while receiving information, artifacts, biological evidence, fingerprints, and patterns. Persons control hosting scenes, and cars to move about. Person scenes instigate ideas and initiate actions while in constant motion, acting and reacting with all scene types. They alter the world around them, and collect evidence while also creating it and sometimes destroying it. Person scenes act central to the case, as the subject and object scenes, the originators, and receivers.

B. Functions. Person scenes function as the ideas and action controlling scene interactions.

1. Mechanical Functions. Person scenes occupy roles as unique action scenes controlling, manipulating, and impacting all other scenes. A person scene controls and alters all other scenes by performing actions to create and retain evidence. Involved persons serve as anchor scenes, with links connecting them with other scenes, and witnesses play an important peripheral role. Person scenes alone have motives to pursue crimes, and those motives often connect with creating evidence. An investigator treats animals like person scenes. They resemble persons as thinking and acting scenes with DNA capable of identifying them.

2. Legal Functions. Person scenes anchor any investigation at the suspect and victim ends. Persons think, choose, and act within the scenes, using scenes to get what they want from another person. Investigators support allegations of persons committing crimes by using evidence to support their connections with actions and outcomes.

C. Structure. Person scenes have defined structure from their design purpose to protect themselves.

1. Restrictions. Persons have barriers surrounding their body, such as clothing, shoes, gloves, hats, or condoms. A person restricts access to his DNA and finger-

prints by taking steps to protect them during his time interacting with other scenes. In contrast the body sloughs off biological evidence all the time, and while the suspect reduces spillage, he cannot eliminate DNA from leaving his control. Smarter suspects increase their own scene restrictions by wearing hats, gloves, condoms, heavy clothing, bullet resistant clothing, and exercising discipline to interact with as few scenes as possible, while taking their evidence with them.

2. Layers. Person scenes come in layers which dictate some of the restrictions. A person has covering like clothing and shoes, the exterior such as hair and fingerprints, the interior such as blood and biological material. Person scenes have at least two, and sometimes three or more layers. Person scenes use their features, in all three layers to manipulate the scenes around him.

3. Interaction Points. Person scenes have many predictable interaction points. Most human bodies have similar features and components.

a. Heads have a high concentration of interaction points to trap evidence including hair, skin, eyes, nose, and mouths with mucous membranes.

b. Most persons use hands to manipulate the environment and control the scenes during crime interactions.

c. Genitals, breasts, and the anus have interactions with other scenes in some crimes.

d. Persons use their feet as means to move, and sometimes as weapons.

e. The rest of the body also interacts with other scenes, insulated by a clothing layer.

f. Most drugs altering the central nervous system interact with the body by affecting the respiration rates, pupil dilation, heart rates, blood pressure, speed of thought and reaction time, balance and coordination.

g. Drugs alter the breath, tongue coloration, nasal lining, and skin from injection sites, also called tracks.

4. Carrying Capacity. The body scene has a high carrying capacity, as a person interacts with other scenes in many different ways and many times a day. The hair, skin, orifices, and clothing all collect evidence in different ways. Persons have the ability to alter their carrying capacity by using exterior covering to form a barrier between the person and other scenes. The layers prevent the suspect's evidence from leaving his person, and capture evidence from scenes the person interacted with.

a. Size of Interaction Area. Person scenes have limited sized interaction areas but simplify investigations. Many of the human body has specialized parts like hands, sex organs, and eyes. Body covering like clothing acts as extensions of the person scene with less defined sizes, but still correlated with the body parts.

b. Material. The human body has mostly soft tissue and hair. Body fluids may collect more evidence, and wash some away. Clothing may soak up some evidence.

c. Topography. The human body has crevices like fingernail beds, cavities like the mouth, and hair to collect evidence. Clothing adds more places to hold evidence.

5. Volatility. Person scenes in perpetual motion create high volatility destroying evidence along the way. The body has soft surfaces along with crevices and hair to collect evidence. Persons flee and change their appearance making them more volatile scenes. If a person already has permanent features saved in a database like DNA or fingerprints the historical record offsets some of their volatility.

III. Scene Investigation

A. Scene Priority Decision. The investigator chooses an involved person (suspect or victim) scene as the priority when it has a high likelihood of evidence connecting it with other scenes in the case. The role indicates persons have the best opportunity for evidence although persons destroy evidence all the time, making them volatile scenes to prove cases. The combination of features makes persons the highest priority scene, even with their varying roles in centrality and proximity.

1. Centrality. The suspect or victim person scenes occupy opposite ends of a chain of scenes and evidence connecting them. They may have evidence of the other, but often has insulation from their polar opposite in the form of other scenes. Person scenes may not have roles as hubs for evidence to connect the chain.

2. Proximity. The person scenes may have high proximity to the crime and even if they are not central to the evidence they may provide evidence of the other end of the chain.

B. Scene Management. The investigator can manage some person scenes easier than others. Persons move about all the time and the investigator must work fast to collect any possible evidence.

1. Isolation. Investigators find person scenes challenging to secure and isolate. Persons think, assess, and act all the time, things which change them as scenes. A person in custody has access to water in a jail cell, paper, and bedding to use to taint the body as a crime scene.

2. Legal Search. Persons present reasons for the investigation to search them. The investigator decides the appropriate way to search the scene within the law. Persons pose a threat to anyone including the investigator. Persons have evidence relevant to the case. The investigator considers safety and the case with upholding the rights of persons. The investigator needs the person's permission, an exigence, an arrest, or search warrant to search a person scene. Victims comply with requests to search their person, while suspects require the investigator obtain authorization by judge, or have reasons for exigency. The courts scrutinize the legality of searches and judges exclude information from sources unlawful to

search. An investigator who violates a suspect's Miranda Rights finds the statement excluded from court as fruit from the poisonous tree.

DNA and biological material from a person scene's legal admissibility rest on the investigator obtaining the samples for sequencing within the law. People discard their material all the time, and investigators sequence person's garbage all the time. Those identifications only goes so far, and the investigator uses a preliminary match as support to obtain a warrant to collect more material in search of a definitive match under heavy legal control.

3. Physical Search. Persons have universal zones simplifying the search of them. Certain areas of the body require specialists or outside experts to investigate for expert opinions interpreting the evidence.

C. Evidence Plan. Working a person scene has all the complexity of other scenes with the additional challenge of a person thinks, acts, and reacts to other scenes and dynamics.

Person scenes sometimes require a higher level of expertise than an officer can provide. Sexual assaults, crimes against children, and death cases all involve medical experts performing specialized investigations like a post-mortem or autopsy, Sexual Assault Response Team exam (SART). An autopsy serves to establish the deceased's identity, how cause and manner of how the person died, and when. The sexual assault exam seeks evidence supporting or refuting a sexual assault. The investigator coordinates those medicolegal investigations with the experts and limits his investigation into the person to information and basic photographs.

For all other cases involving person scenes, the investigator's method follows the pattern of other scenes.

1. Information.

a. Observations. Investigators have more opportunities to observe persons as time goes on, and they conduct searches. Removing layers of clothing exposes more areas for the investigator. The investigator will have many observations pertaining to the person's appearance, smell, actions, and statements.

b. Statements. The investigator can ask follow up questions of persons to clarify conditions, and evidence.

c. Measurements. Person scene investigations can require precise measurements such as height and weight. Detailed measurements provide objectivity in an area of subjective statements.

d. History. Person scenes have files of information in many locations. The Department of Motor Vehicles often serves as the identification bureau with descriptions and photographs of persons, along with their address and connection with cars. Criminal justice files indicate if a person has DNA on file in CODIS or if the person has prior arrests or law enforcement encounters. Some DNA testing services have a person's DNA on file, or DNA of a family member of the person. Autopsies performed by medical examiners provide specialized person scene investigations. Sexual assaults also have dedicated trained nurses to perform examinations. With these outside sub investigations, the investigator limits his investigation to preliminary information and photographs.

2. Photographs.

a. Investigator. The investigator takes pictures of persons at the hosting scenes. The investigator takes photographs early in the investigation and the collection of photographs includes anyone with any connection to the case. Detailed images come after meeting the base requirement of documentation. The investigator's postcrime photographs show the impact of crime interactions on the person, or to show emotional impact, or sometimes for identification.

b. Citizens. Persons may take photographs before, during, or after a crime showing the person. The investigator obtains these images from the person, or finds them online at a photo sharing site. A cooperative person provides a historical photo of him or herself. Hosting scenes may have cameras watching over the area a person occupied. Police agencies have recording devices on employees to capture audio and video footage of police action. Historical photographs come from the internet or a justice system if a person has a prior arrest history.

3. Artifacts.

a. Objects. Persons collect material evidence from their interactions with other scenes. Person scenes wear clothing, which have pockets, and in many cases a person's pockets contain everything from receipts providing timestamped locational data, as well as purchase information. The investigator treats a person's tools also as artifacts under some circumstances.

b. Trace. Person scenes also collect small material, such as dust, lint, leaves, or dirt from hosting scenes, called trace evidence.

4. Biological Material.

a. Serology. Most scenes hold biological material covered by serology and DNA. Only person scenes (and all animal scene analogs) create DNA and distribute it with biological material such as skin cells, hair, body fluids, and fingernails. Asymmetric interaction points contact each other, such as oral genital contact providing biological material of different origins, such as semen and saliva.

The investigator uses the initial information to choose what tests to conduct. A burglary suspect requires fewer processing steps than a sexual assault suspect. Executing a burglary requires a person use hands and feet, while a sexual assault also requires hands and feet and other body areas like the sex organs, and mouth.

b. DNA. Person scenes create their own DNA and collect other persons' DNA as they interact with those scenes. Most persons have the same interaction points. Every area of the body produces and sheds DNA laden cells, but the interaction points such as the genitals with semen or vaginal fluid, and the mouth with saliva produce and have a carrying fluid. The human body produces DNA inside and on the exterior surface. DNA exists on three layers of a person scene: the covering, the exterior, and the interior. The body's covering and exterior layers have the highest propensity for interactions with other scenes. Those layers hold discarded DNA from the person, ready to share. A person performs a secondary transfer of DNA from his clothing, hair, or skin to another scene. Counterforensics like hats, gloves, and condoms prevent or reduce the person's scene from discarding DNA. A person's interior also holds another person's biological material and DNA such as in in orifices and cavities.

5. Fingerprints.

a. Latent. A person receiving another person's fingerprints cleans the prints off with constant motion. A person scene carries fingerprints on their covering layer such as on clothing like metal belt buckles. Skin has the capability to accept and preserve a fingerprint, but living bodies move around, often destroying the evidence. Dead persons fall under the control of the Medical Examiner and staff, so if an investigator wants a fingerprint she must coordinate with the ME before moving the body and destroying evidence.

b. Patent. A person and clothing can accept patent fingerprints in mediums such as blood or paint.

c. Plastic. Person scenes do not have soft material able to take an impression of a fingerprint and preserve it, so any plastic prints come from outside mediums.

6. Pattern Marks

a. Visual Physical. The human body accepts a wide variety of visual and physical patterns. Tools make patterns when trauma bruises flesh and breaks bones. The seatbelt and steering wheel impart patterns from car parts onto a person. A person using his teeth as tools leaves dental patterns or bite marks on the scene. DNA supplants the need to use bite mark evidence, but the pattern mark remains after a victim has showered, and washed away the DNA. Most persons wear shoes and have the potential to leave shoe tread marks, or pattern marks where they step. Person scenes also take on the pattern of a scene which the person remained in contact with for a long time, such as textures.

b. Chemical. Investigators use chemical patterns to show exposure to particular chemical formulas, such as drug residue, or accelerant residue for a fire setting suspect.

c. Information. A person scene provides information, and the investigator gathers more information about the scene during the investigation. Some of the information comes in pattern form, such as a person's descriptions for alerts. If the case hinges on information only a few persons have access to, then the information patterns of access, signatures, or authentication play a part.

CHAPTER 3. EVIDENCE WORK

The decisive investigator decides how to obtain the evidence from the scenes and what it means. The investigator looks at three areas of evidence: collection, creation, and proof ability to analyze it.

The investigator applies those three areas to the six evidence types of information, photographs, artifacts, biological material, fingerprints, and pattern marks. The order of these thematic investigations comes from how they present to the investigator and what the investigator does in order to investigate the scene get the most from it.

How to work evidence?

Evidence comes to the investigator as direct evidence proving facts and indirect evidence proving conditions. The evidence also comes as either physical evidence or documentary evidence. Documentary evidence provides a representation of other evidence. This secondary evidence or meta-evidence stands in for immovable or unavailable physical evidence. Evidence collection depends on where the investigator finds it. Analyzing what it means and how got there come in the next chapter of evidence analysis. Each evidence type has divisions.

Goal. The investigator seeks to find, collect, and process evidence and then convert it from raw evidence to proof and facts relating to proving who did what.

I. Evidence Collection

Each evidence type requires specific skills, but the investigator can apply the skills to any scene with minor adjustments. Each type of evidence has a collection of different sub types. Collection hinges on skills, technology, and admissibility.

A. Find. Each evidence type has origins specific to it. A solid scene analysis sets the investigator on the right course for gathering evidence. Every piece of evidence has a scene source combining location, physics, and evidence properties.

1. Persons. Involved persons create and hold evidence. No matter how many scenes separating suspect and victim, one initiates and takes actions causing a chain reaction which reaches the other person. Witnesses observe crime outside the chain reaction.

2. Places. Places receive evidence from interactions of scenes. Suspects, victims, and witnesses control subordinate scenes, and impact scenes outside their control.

3. Things. Objects also receive evidence the same ways as places from suspects, victims, and witnesses.

4. Dynamics. The investigator may collect evidence about an event instead of a physical entity.

B. Extract. Each evidence type has its own set of skills an investigator uses to obtain the evidence, and each sub type. The investigator needs gloves, hats, particle masks, and booties protect the evidence and the investigator during collection.

C. Preserve. Each evidence type has its own ways to preserve it.

D. Process. Collected raw evidence often requires additional processing to convert it to usable information. Some evidence requires little processing, but some evidence requires trained experts. The processes can vary a great deal within the type of evidence. Laboratory technicians or criminalists work with the evidence to obtain proof from it.

1. Refine. Most evidence comes from the source in a raw form. Someone refines it to a usable form.

2. Standardize. The investigator or technician must standardize the evidence to compare it with other evidence.

3. Interpret. The investigator interprets the evidence on a simple level, but may rely on the expert to interpret the results of evidence processing.

The investigator processes some evidence, but also forwards evidence to laboratories for greater expertise. The American Society of Crime Laboratory Directors (ASCLaD) certifies labs to verify they are using accepted procedure for evidence handling and processing.

E. Technical Admissibility. Judges determine if a piece of evidence has scientific backing to prove its point in court. Courts want to ensure the investigator collected the evidence and protected it for reliability. The courts evaluate scientific evidence by Frye or Daubert. Frye applies to some states. Daubert applies to some states and the US Supreme Court, making it the ultimate evaluation form if the case goes far enough. Both court decisions create tests to ensure the reliability of scientific based evidence, artifacts and opinions about evidence under the standard of the scientific method. Evidence must come from a tested method with standards and subject to peer review with a majority of the scientific community's acceptance. It must have a known potential error rate. The investigator proves the evidence discovery, collection, and refinement processes reproducible with the same results. Most departments provide policy guidance on technical procedures. Court fights often center on the investigator's adherence to policy and current accepted practices as a way to determine if he conducted the procedures in accordance with the approved scientific ways.

F. Legal Admissibility. Judges also determine if an investigator collected a piece of evidence in accordance with the law. This relates back to the lawful search of a scene. Courts rule violations of Constitutional Rights to freedom from unlawful search and seizure, or coerced statements as excluded from trial unless obtained under exceptional circumstances like the safety exception.

II. Evidence Analysis

Proving what happened in cases comes from understanding the processes for creating evidence. Crime scene physics make evidence as a result of scene interactions. How scenes make evidence becomes important once the investigator has discovered it. Creation involves synthesis, cause and vulnerabilities.

A. Cause. Every piece of evidence comes into existence as the effect from some cause. When the investigator can determine the cause behind the evidence it moves the case closer to solving. Evidence has five major causes: intentional, accidental, functional, habitual, and byproduct, and the often lead to persons.

1. Intentional Evidence. Intentional scene interactions create an intended evidence result, like building a bomb.

2. Accidental Evidence. An unintended consequence of scene interactions, like a crashed car from driving while intoxicated creates accidental evidence.

3. Functional Evidence. The interaction of scenes in a process to achieve a function creates evidence, like a forged check.

4. Habitual Evidence. When a person performs routine tasks it creates evidence of presence and actions, like spitting tobacco in a crime scene.

5. Byproduct Evidence. When the interactions of scenes create evidence related to the crime, but not at the center of the crime they create byproduct evidence, like broken glass from a window used as an entry point for a burglary.

B. Creation. Matter becomes evidence when it has a role in a case, but evidence happens by construction, deconstruction and transfer.

1. Construction. Evidence results from one scene combining with another. A person's fingerprints on a knife used to stab another person resulting in a bloody knife make a constructed piece of evidence of three parts. The overall evidence of the bloody knife with fingerprints has several transfers: the knife from storage scene to the person scene, the fingerprints from the person scene to the knife, the

blood of the person to the knife, and the person transferring the knife to its new storage place. Construction of matter may precede transformation into evidence.

2. Deconstruction. Evidence breaks apart during crimes, a part of a scene transfers from one scene to another. During a fight a person scratches another person, and lodges the person's flesh and skin under his fingernails.

3. Transfer. Evidence moves between scenes during the course of a crime, and can change possessors. Transfer converts preexisting matter into evidence.

a. The suspect, victim, or third party introduces the evidence from elsewhere.

b. The suspect, victim, or third party introduces the evidence by choosing it from the same hosting scene.

c. The suspect, victim, or third party creates the evidence in the hosting scene.

d. The suspect controlled the evidence and retained control throughout the event.

e. The suspect controlled the evidence and lost control of it during the event.

f. The victim controlled the evidence and retained control throughout the event.

g. The victim controlled the evidence and lost control of it during the event.

4. Complications. Most investigations have lag time between the crime and the case work. Even when investigators witness the crime they have lag time relating to perceiving the case.

a. The suspect, victim, third party may have possession of evidence and leave the evidence in the hosting scene.

b. The suspect, victim, third party may have possession and take the evidence from the hosting scene.

c. Sometimes the actions or environmental conditions of the crime destroy evidence, such as a fire or weather.

III. Evidence to Proof

The investigator uses each piece of evidence's characteristics and its situation to determine its capability to prove facts. Evidence context or orientation helps the investigator understand how it fits in with the other elements. Proof ability comes last in analyzing evidence as the investigator must have the evidence, and know its history before knowing what it means. Evidence has strengths and weaknesses.

A. Strengths. The evidence's strength to prove important facts determines its value in a case.

1. Accuracy. Evidence provides detailed or limited facts of identification, presence, action, control, and damage. Evidence may prove more than one aspect. Evidence's nearness to the actual facts relates to its accuracy. Accurate measurements have closeness to the right answer, while precise measurements show a consistency for being close to each other over multiple times. Some evidence

provides precise answers, and other general information in need of companion evidence to support it.

2. Uniqueness. The more unique the evidence, the stronger the evidence. Fingerprints and DNA provide more unique identification than a statement description of a person being a white male, wearing a red shirt and blue jeans.

3. Proof Ability. Evidence proves facts, and the closer it comes to proving who did what, the more valuable. A knife with suspect DNA on the handle, and victim DNA in the blood on the blade provides greater proof ability than a witness statement placing a suspect in the area.

B. Weaknesses. Every evidence type has limitations. Each evidence piece provides part of the proof with voids for the investigator to fill.

1. Vulnerability. All evidence has vulnerabilities damaging its usefulness in a case. Investigators often measure vulnerability weakness by time as all evidence degrades or changes over time.

a. Environment. The weather or scene surrounding the evidence makes it vulnerable to alteration or destruction, as well as follow on transfer.

b. Persons. Persons alter or destroy evidence without intention. Well-meaning persons trample through and clean scenes all the time.

2. Countermeasures. Evidence includes vulnerabilities, and many times suspects engage in countermeasures during crimes to reduce the evidence opportunities. Suspects practice discipline like wearing gloves. They also take additional actions on the victim scenes and evidence to reduce usable evidence.

3. Proof Inability. No piece of evidence can do all things. Many evidence types have significant inabilities for the investigator to notice and work around.

C. Evidence Strengthening. Even with vulnerabilities and suspect countermeasures, investigators can build strong cases by reinforcing the evidence.

1. Documentation. Technical experts provide key general information to explain events or processes for an investigator to include in the report. The expert's statement explains novel and foreign concepts to investigators and juries alike. The expert also explains specific evidence items in regards to procedures.

2. Corroboration. Most evidence relies on other evidence to create context and validity while shoring it up.

3.1 WORKING INFORMATION

Information evidence distills facts about all evidence. The investigator uses a formatted version of information seeking early in an investigation to take it from case to scene, and evaluates evidence at the end of the book to prove the case. This section covers the complete area of information in its four types:

3.1.1 Observations

3.1.2 Statements.

3.1.3 Measurements.

3.1.4 Historical.

Goal. The investigator seeks information as evidence about evidence to provide a baseline of facts in an investigation.

3.1.1 WORKING OBSERVATIONS

The investigator makes first person observations of details throughout the case to build baseline information.

Goal. The investigator seeks to observe details about scenes, and evidence to use as stand-alone or contributing facts in the case.

I. Evidence Collection

A. Find. The investigator proceeds with caution in the early phases of an investigation to avoid destroying the evidence she does not yet know exists. An investigator makes observations from the earliest awareness to the end of the case as nonimpact evidence gathering. Investigators observe scenes, evidence, and actions as evidence; straight from the scene, and from peripheral sources. The most common observations collect basic information.

1. Persons. Investigators note a person's appearance, and actions from the introduction.

2. Places. Investigators observe places by noting the size, appearance, and functions.

3. Things. Investigators collect similar observations from things as from place such as their size, appearance, and function.

B. Extract. Investigators often define evidence by observation about class characteristics and individual characteristics. Observations are things the investigator senses and records. While investigators are trained observers, anyone can question their observations for accuracy and precision, as they might another witness. Observations from what the investigator sees approaching, at the scene, and when leaving. Investigators observe scenes including persons and record those observations. Investigators notice damage easier than less obvious evidence carrying interaction points. Measuring scenes with accuracy and precision shows objective details of distances and differences. The investigator records observations relating all senses. A description covers details, and what makes the particular scene of observation unique. Objectivity and remaining with the facts makes strong observations.

C. Preserve. The investigator preserves observations first in notes, and then in the report.

D. Process. Observations require little processing.

1. Refine. The observations may require the addition of details like times and locations of observations.

2. Standardize. The investigator standardizes observations by defining as much as possible and noting things like distances, lighting, and anything a person may want to know about.

3. Interpret. The investigator should define facts, and assumptions. Describing a person with a red stained shirt works covers the facts without assuming the red stains blood stains.

E. Technical Admissibility. Courts admit observations but they also come under heavy scrutiny by an opposing attorney in court.

F. Legal Admissibility. Courts admit investigator's observations assuming the investigator had a legal right to presence in a place to make the observation.

II. Evidence Analysis

A. Cause. The investigator observes most evidence by intention and accident.

B. Creation. The investigator creates observation evidence by alertness and transferring what he could experience into what he could record.

III. Evidence to Proof

A. Strengths. The investigator can use information observation evidence to build facts from proof.

1. Accuracy. Persons can make accurate observations, investigator or citizen. Observations focusing on a detail or two may have specific information for the investigation.

2. Uniqueness. Persons observing scenes, evidence, and events can find the unique parts and note them.

3. Proof Ability. An investigator's observations have strong proof ability given the position of trust the public attributes to him. First impression observations form a baseline of facts with the expectation of verification.

B. Weaknesses. Information observation evidence comes from the parts of scenes, evidence, and dynamics a person experienced.

1. Vulnerability. A person must have the position to observe, and a person can question anyone's accuracy. A person records observations, but they lack hard evidence. The investigator's observations combine to a group of circumstances. Observations can seem like opinion statements with the wrong expressions. Noting a person's tears documents an observation. Analyzing for deeper meanings wastes time, and exposes the investigator as an amateur psychologist.

2. Countermeasures. Suspects can engage in countermeasures to scenes and evidence to reduce the odds of capture. The suspect often flees as the primary way to reduce observations by the investigator. He may take things with him, and alter stationary scenes.

3. Proof Inability. A person must notice something for an observation. Investigators miss things and sometimes observing a scene, evidence, or dynamic cannot prove a theory like hard evidence can.

C. Evidence Strengthening. Investigator observations alone can have limited value to a case. Any evidence to corroborate the observations fills the voids, even if only photographs.

3.1.2 WORKING STATEMENTS

The investigator collects statements of persons, including their observations, with the information goal of establishing a baseline of who, what, where, when, why, and how.

Goal. The investigator seeks statements from persons connected with the case to provide insight into evidence and scenes contributing provable facts to the case.

I. Evidence Collection

A. Find. The investigator obtains statements from persons connected with a case. Statements gather up a person's observations about things. Statements come from persons only.

B. Extract. The investigator's skills to extract statement information require discipline and patience. Digital audio and video recordings preserve the exact details of the information and its presentation. Keeping notes also helps for report writing. The investigator seeks multiple statements from many people at different times during the investigation to clarify the information and identify locations of evidence. The purest information comes from early statements when the person focuses on the events and entities in them. Time allows a person to rationalize and consider meanings and reasons. Those may help a case, but evidence solves a case.

Interviews obtain information from only person scenes. Interviewing more persons early and in the hosting scene present opportunities for corroborating evidence comes soon after. Most cases have the investigator interviewing some persons at the outset. Most cases also have the investigator interviewing persons later for more details. In the limited scope of this book interviewing reduces to its basic functions of rapport, questions, and clarification.

a. Rapport. The investigator should make the person comfortable enough to speak about the matter. The investigator should ease a person into speaking about what happened.

b. Questions. Open ended questions earn responses in the interviewee's own words. The right questions can help the person get to precise statements while still in the person's own words. The investigator may ask a few questions the person has no answer for. While frustrating, it also shows the extent of the person's knowledge, and the investigator obtained as much as possible, while remaining with factual information. Most person talk in a casual tone, with familiarity, so the investigator has to keep the information coming while also clarifying specific details of who, what, where, when, why, and how. What people say varies in accuracy and usefulness. Proving who said what proves little compared to proving who did what.

c. Clarification. When the person finishes, the investigator can ask open ended questions to clarify such as asking to hear more about an aspect of the case. If the information lacks the details the investigator can ask yes or no questions.

The investigator should interview a person alone to avoid influence. Statements require a back and forth method. The investigator should also understand how the Miranda Warning works and decide how to approach it. Interrogation involves other techniques not covered in this book.

Departments have protocols for when the statement includes identifying a person in a line up. The witness should only identify a person based on prior observations.

Sometimes persons make spontaneous statements. These statements come from a person without prompting or questioning, such as a person blurting out at a death scene, "I was only trying to scare him!" These emotion driven statements often support cases with strong evidence. The investigator must prepare for these unexpected yet key pieces of information evidence by recording as soon as stepping out of the car.

C. Preserve. The investigator preserves a summary of information evidence in written form as a report. The investigator also preserves the raw information in audio and digital recordings.

D. Process. Statement information often comes in a large amount of information where the investigator must pick out the key points.

1. Refine. The investigator must know what the person making the statement said.

2. Standardize. The investigator ensures the statement refers to relevant parts of the case.

3. Interpret. The investigator works with facts of the statement to interpret what they mean.

E. Technical Admissibility. The courts can and will question a statement in cross examination as part of the effort to validate the person making the statement can talk about the case in a meaningful way.

F. Legal Admissibility. The courts require the investigator obtain statements in a lawful manner by having a legal right to speak with a person, and obtain statements without coercion. Offers of deals and breaks result in exclusion of statements.

II. Evidence Analysis

A. Cause. Statement information evidence comes mostly from intentional actions on the part of the person making the statement. Spontaneous statements come about by accident.

B. Creation. Persons construct their statements by observing scenes, evidence, and actions.

III. Evidence to Proof

A. Strengths. Statement information evidence can help build a baseline and indicate other evidence.

1. Accuracy. Statement information connects scenes, evidence, and events by covering a period of time. Most statement evidence varies from general, to specific points. Many times persons focus on particular areas, recalling fine details.

2. Uniqueness. Persons can make statements providing unique information if the investigator asks the right open ended questions, and follows up to clarify.

3. Proof Ability. A person willing to swear the truthfulness of a statement has some proof ability, subject to verification. Information evidence provides the baseline in most cases of simple statements, an officer's observations, and a few historical references. The investigator considers if and how the information corroborates other information, evaluating it against other evidence. The investigator compares statements to facts from the other evidence to build the case, and determine witnesses' reliability. Persons with connections to involved parties like suspects and victims may have an interest in the case outcome. The investigator overcomes the situation by corroborating the information and using the interviews and interrogations of persons close to the action to help find other evidence. Evidence proves facts of the case and corroborates the statement. A suspect or victim may have difficulty providing an unbiased statement, while a third party witness who observed events gives a neutral and factual statement. The investigator verifies those facts by other sources and evidence types. Persons estimate times, distances, and most other measurements. A lack of precision requires a noted margin of error or at least a qualifying statement of approximation. Eyewitness accounts have fallibility. Information provides the investigator the first introduction to a case. He arrives and gets a synopsis from an involved party or another investigator. The first information a person learns has huge influence over his ideas about the case playing into a bias. When investigators turn information into evidence without

verification it creates a false sense of the case. Alleged facts about a case remain allegations without proof. A suspect's confession requires the investigator corroborate the statement with facts.

B. Weaknesses. Statements have built in weaknesses in their ability to prove actual events and condition. Evidence about evidence cannot prove the same things as the primary evidence. Juries prefer identification by physical evidence over statements.

1. Vulnerability. Cases relying on statement information have high vulnerability. The source person can forget or change a statement and sometimes adding or removing facts. Like observations, statements have the human factor making them vulnerable to problems like the source's perspective, emotions, and objectivity. Persons have limitations to how long they can remember details and to what lever of precision. Person-sourced information from statements vary in accuracy subject to heavy scrutiny in court. A person's statements have a high level of risk for accuracy as they may not have correct details or vary over time, making them imprecise. Statements have relative low accuracy compared with a photograph, but statements can provide combinations of details. Time creates more challenges for statement information, as persons forget and downgrade their accuracy and precision of facts.

2. Countermeasures. Persons can provide evasive and meaningless statements as a way to compromise some investigations with bad information. Persons lie and omit facts. Influence can impact another person's statements by threat of force or fear.

3. Proof Inability. Statements rely on a person recalling observations about scenes, evidence, and dynamics. Statements do not prove facts like hard evidence can.

C. Evidence Strengthening. Original evidence provides the best proof, and any corroborating evidence. Information evidence provides partial proof toward facts by providing background and context to other evidence.

1. Documentation. Some statement information evidence stands alone, but most of it acts as meta evidence about other evidence so the investigator strengthens the case by covering the background of the statements. Tying the statements to facts helps strengthen them. Recording reduces the vulnerability of statements.

2. Corroboration. Information evidence pairs well with any other evidence. Statement information is evidence about evidence. Gathered statements indicating a dynamic of scenes and evidence also require corroboration by hard evidence.

3.1.3 WORKING MEASUREMENTS

The investigator collects measurements of scenes and evidence to define them.

Goal. The investigator seeks measurements of scenes and evidence as precise observations contributing provable facts to the case.

I. Evidence Collection

A. Find. Investigators take measurements of all manner of scenes, evidence, and dynamics.

1. Persons. Investigators collect various measurements from persons such as distances, weights, pulse, and respiration rates.

2. Places. Investigators collect measurements from places like heights, widths, volumes, lighting, and even air quality.

3. Things. Investigators collect measurement from objects such as dimensions, and weight.

4. Dynamics. Investigators measure dynamics in time, distances, and forces.

B. Extract. Measurements are observations with built in objectivity, as a measuring device observes factual information on a common scale. Measurements apply to all scene types. The investigator's measurements are calibrated observations. Larger items have larger units of measure, and smaller items have smaller units. Nature has few straight lines, and fewer right angles, and tools put nature on a universal scale. The investigator uses tape measures, laser measures, rolling tape measures, documents the tool used to measure in the report including relevant calibration details. Scenes require both long and short distance measurements. The investigator also takes measurements involving larger numbers as the scenes can take more space. Outdoor scenes have maps and satellite imagery available on the internet, to use to create sketches. Investigators overlay key evidence locations onto images, or create new sketches to gather key information depicting locations and distances of key artifacts.

C. Preserve. The investigator preserves information evidence in written form as a report or in sketches. Photographs augment the written documentation.

D. Process. Measurements require information what the investigator measure, how, and what tool he used to determine the measurement.

1. Refine. The investigator seeks high accuracy and specificity.

2. Standardize. The investigator should form the measurement information in a report following conventions of order to keep it organized. Measurements require orientation information to make them meaningful.

3. Interpret. The investigator works with many measurement facts to interpret what they mean but often limits interpretation of measurement facts.

E. Technical Admissibility. Measurements have high court room admissibility, but like observations and statements opposition seeks to validate or discredit them by method or results.

F. Legal Admissibility. The investigator must measurements in a lawful manner to have them in court.

II. Evidence Analysis

A. Cause. The investigator takes all measurements with intention. What the investigator measures such as distances and location may result from any of the five causes of evidence creation: intentional, accidental, functional, habitual, and byproduct.

B. Creation. The investigator considers a scene's construction, deconstruction, or transfer of evidence to measures scenes, evidence, and dynamics.

III. Evidence to Proof

A. Strengths. Information measurement evidence can have high strength when measurement requires little skill.

1. Accuracy. Measurements and have greater accuracy if the investigator uses good tools to measure and record observations, while estimates can have low accuracy.

2. Uniqueness. The investigators measurements can show the uniqueness in scenes, and evidence by recording the exact composition of it.

3. Proof Ability. An investigator's measurements come with high proof ability. The collection of most measurements has low technical requirements. The investigator's measurements show construction details, scene limitations, and potential options like forced choices within the scenes. Factual measurements of a 250 pound person fighting a 120 pound person present a mental picture of the differ-

ences between the two combatants. Information provides contextual orientation and timelines such as when a person left home, when he returned to find it burgled, and when he called 911. Those three information points fit on a measured timeline. A large or small gap between leaving and returning home has little significance, but an investigator requires an explanation for large gap between discovering a crime and reporting it.

B. Weaknesses. Measurements depend on the yardstick and techniques for accuracy.

1. Vulnerability. The investigator can incorrectly measure scenes and evidence. Information evidence should have few weaknesses assuming the investigator followed procedure in taking them.

2. Countermeasures. Suspects can move things or destroy scenes to ruin measurements.

3. Proof Inability. Measurements cannot prove all parts of an equation like whether a person could travel a certain distance in a time. Measurements have high rationality, but persons may make decisions for different reasons.

C. Evidence Strengthening. The investigator's measurements often quire photographs like the observations to show the values.

1. Documentary. Photographing the scene and measurement device documents the evidence process.

2. Corroboration. Scaled photographs and background information help support the measurements.

3.1.4 WORKING HISTORICAL INFORMATION

The investigator collects historical information details of the case as external based facts to build the information about a case.

Goal. The investigator seeks to learn historical details about scenes and evidence to use as stand-alone or contributing facts in the case.

I. Evidence Collection

A. Find. The investigator obtains historical information sources able to hold details. Historical evidence can vary from the truth, a suspect's history, or victim's history. Many times historical information can involve informational pattern matching as covered in section 6.3 of this chapter.

1. Places. Investigators collect historical information from archives, libraries, and halls of records. This includes websites, social networking sites, the phone company, and internet service providers (ISP).

2. Things. Investigators collect historical information from things like computers, books, rap sheets, websites, or records.

B. Extract. The investigator may mine a great deal of historical information by knowing what to search and the right search skills. While vetted information has high reliability, it is only as good as the information entered in. Historical information requires access to databases.

a. Government Databases. Most government based investigations provide access to government databases. This searching requires a name, date of birth, location, case number, or identifying features such as scars, marks, or tattoos. The DMV provides information about who has a driver's license at a residence, and who has registered what cars there. The National Crime Information Center (NCIC), criminal justice computers also provide some of the same information, and information about persons' criminal history, associates, and cars as they relate to crime. Technicians search CODIS (Combined DNA Indexing System) by DNA or by person. An investigator can search IAFIS (Integrated Automatic Fingerprint Identification System) by name or print of person.

b. Private Databases. The investigator can often glean far more details from commercial databases than government databases. Private companies have a profit motive for them to collect and store information. Private databases have more information about persons, connections the person has to relatives, phone numbers, and internet sources. They cover what the person owns, and controls, along with activities such as civil actions. Insurance companies provide information about the person's history with insurance, from claims to lawsuits. Insurance companies have extensive databases which can provide a trove of information about persons, cars, and properties. Any website with a signup requirement gathers information about the person who signed up, and can provide details. A supermarket card can provide details like timestamped locations. An investigator can search private databases by name, address, phone number, or email address, or internet handle.

c. Public Databases. The internet provides information, specifications, and images for anything. Like other information evidence, the investigator must consider the source since public databases can reflect the views of the controller. The internet also provides mapping and satellite imagery. Real estate websites have detailed information including floor plans, and interior photographs. Guns have diagrams on the internet for the investigator annotate with evidence locations, and a ruler scale. Most investigators first identify drugs by appearance and their context of packaging and storage. County databases cover property deeds, Deeds of Trust, liens and civil suits associated with assets. Investigators have a harder time associating anonymous renters with private scenes, but many searchable private databases have the information. Sometimes investigators have access to utilities such as water. The investigator can search public databases by name, locations, email address, internet handle, and in some cases a photo.

d. Archives. Some places have not put their records online accessible from anywhere, and require a person to visit. Some local governments have hard copy files or microfiche accessible along with clerks available to help search by name, address, date of event or birth, or any other field. Archives also include bank records, which require an account holder's permission or a search warrant for the investigator access.

e. Books. The investigator will probably not use a lot of books, but they can provide fast information for things like identifying drugs by number. Searching books involves the table of contents or index.

C. Preserve. The investigator preserves historical information evidence in written form as a report, and if possible the original record. Sometimes a digital copy, photocopy, or image suffices.

D. Process. Once the investigator has the historical information she must process it to make it useful. If the information resides in a machine or tool, a technician may process the device to get the evidence.

1. Refine. The investigator finds relevant information and narrows it down to specific points.

2. Standardize. The investigator forms information into comparable facts another person could use to draw conclusions. Some historical information comes in a database form where the investigator may have to configure the information in a way to standardize it for use.

3. Interpret. The investigator works historical facts to interpret what they mean in the context of the recent crime.

E. Technical Admissibility. The courts scrutinize how the investigator obtained the historical information to ensure he observed procedure to endure solid evidence.

F. Legal Admissibility. The courts examine historical information to determine if the investigator obtained the evidence with legal authorization and without coercion of the controller of the information.

II. Evidence Analysis

A. Cause. Most historical information evidence preexists the case as an intentional effort to save a record. It can involve accidental saving. In some cases historical evidence records byproduct information about a matter related to the crime in a tangential way.

B. Creation. Someone or something constructs historical information by recording information.

III. Evidence to Proof

A. Strengths. Historical information's strengths can lie in its closeness or distance from the crime.

1. Accuracy. Information predating the case can have greater accuracy from its neutrality. It came about without the pressure of events surrounding the crime. Recorded information has a paper trail for an investigator to validate.

2. Uniqueness. Recorded information about scenes and some evidence provide an opportunity for the investigator to find their uniqueness among the details.

3. Proof Ability. Information from archived sources has high proof ability. It often anchors possession, ownership, and actions. Established sources of information provide strong information, such as the DMV, but historical information has different contexts. A data system also shows presence. Information proves actions by also recording events such as ATM withdrawals, or internet searches. These actions provide time stamps, locational data, and video footage of the event. Records prove ownership, legal possession, and control. Sometimes persons deny connections and records impeach their statements with facts.

B. Weaknesses. Historical information sources can only provide evidence and facts entered into them.

1. Vulnerability. Information can never gain precision or accuracy coming out of an archive and age does not always mean great accuracy. Some other information repositories have little or no structure challenging the investigator's search efforts.

2. Countermeasures. A secure third party often controls historical information posing challenges for suspect countermeasures. Most countermeasures relating to historical information rely on obscuring connections to it, hoping the investigator will not find it, or discrediting the sources.

3. Proof Inability. Historical evidence covers the past, and may not prove anything in an investigation. Information coming from a source like an archive or database only covers what a person entered into it. Out of date or wrong information may present as current and accurate information. The internet at large has no mechanism to validate or vet information.

C. Evidence Strengthening. Historical information evidence has strength in its redundancy and variety of sources without motivation toward crime.

Some information evidence stands alone, but most of it acts as meta evidence about other evidence. Original evidence provides the best proof, and any corroborating evidence. Information evidence provides partial proof toward facts by providing background and context to other evidence. Information evidence pairs well with any other evidence. Historical information often corroborates information about the situation leading to the crime.

1. Documentary. The investigator's coverage of the process of obtaining historical information eliminates many questions in court.

2. Corroboration. The investigator strengthens the evidence when other evidence independent of the studied evidence can provide similar facts and details. The inclusion of hard evidence preceding the recorded information, or other information in the form of a paper trail can verify the information. Historical information disappears or a person rewrites it, so a photograph or print out of historical information protects it

3.2 WORKING PHOTOGRAPHS

Images scenes, evidence, and situations portray matters about evidence including appearances, and locations. Photographs have two types:

3.2.1 Investigator photographs.

3.2.2 Citizen or non-investigator generated.

Goal. The investigator seeks photographs as documentary evidence to show facts in an investigation.

3.2.1 WORKING INVESTIGATOR PHOTOGRAPHS

The investigator takes photographs to memorialize details and facts of the case throughout the investigation.

Goal. The investigator seeks to observe details about scenes and evidence by collecting images to use as stand-alone or contributing facts in the case.

I. Evidence Collection

A. Find. Investigators take photographs for evidence. A photographer works with complex equipment to produce images measured on technical and composition quality. Images, like information evidence, represent the evidence and come from the same sources.

1. Persons. The investigator photographs persons showing appearances and features.

2. Places. The investigator photographs places hosting scenes, evidence, and action.

3. Things. The investigator photographs objects like tools showing the dynamics of crime.

4. Dynamics. The investigator sometimes captures images of outcomes of dynamics, or dynamics contributing to an outcome.

B. Extract. The investigator collects most photographs by taking them. The investigator provides most of the images in a case showing outcomes, and all the parts. High quality images trade showing the actual crime for showing the outcome in high clarity. Photographic evidence shows scenes and situations at a specific point in time. The images show relationships for the investigator to use as circumstances. Every scene has photographable components to show the situation, and sometimes the outcome of the case. Photographs provide context for scenes and evidence as visual information. Digital photographs provide immediate feedback permitting the operator to make adjustments. Sophisticated technology makes technical aspects of photography easier for the photographer.

The investigator also needs gloves to prevent contamination of evidence if he touches it during the photographs.

Photographic evidence constructs a representation of reality. Cameras reproduce two dimensional representation of a three dimensional world. Photographic evidence can provide a way to look at scenes and evidence into specific parts. The camera depicts whatever happens at the moment of capturing the image, whether introduction, control, or closing of involvement. Image size in megapixels and the format of the saved image help determine sharpness of photographs. Larger numbers of pixels mean a higher number of dots making up the image, and more details allowing a person to enlarge photographs and still remain clear. Low pixel numbers makes enlarged photographs grainy, and less clear, lacking enough detail to show license plates from a distance.

1. Technical. An image's technical quality relates to how well the camera captures the image including focus, exposure for the right distance, f/stop or aperture size, shutter speed, and how well the flash works to fill the shadows but avoid washing out the image. Technology still requires skill and knowledge of the basics about how an automated camera works. The camera provides a focused image showing the subject as near to life as possible. If the images involve filters and special lighting to accentuate features, the images record what a person sees using special equipment. The image eliminates the need to view the subject with equipment.

a. Camera. Photographers used to control all the technical aspects of taking pictures. Cameras advanced and those functions became automated controlling the focus, aperture, time of exposure, and flash. Most investigators have moved from film cameras to digital with electronic components and save the image as data in the form of 1's and 0's. Film has higher costs for printed images. A person reviews digital images on a screen for free, email them, and print them for low cost on any printer. The camera takes the image, but requires a lens dependent upon distance from the subject. New cameras can also include GPS data.

b. Flash. Variable lighting requires a flash to fills the shadows and shows all the details.

c. ALS. An alternate light source (ALS) makes some invisible evidence visible expanding the field of visible evidence. The light does not damage the evidence and causes no chemical change. Light waves come in different wavelengths. Specific wavelengths make certain substances stand out, such as semen and fingerprints. The investigator uses colored glasses or photographs with colored filters to make the materials visible. For example, 450 nm light makes bruises and bite marks visible and works well on people with darker skin tones. 485 nm light makes the oil in fingerprints visible. 570 nm light illuminates a variety of material, making it the first light for the process.

d. Scale. Ruler tape or a ruler shows size and scale in images.

e. Tripod. A tripod holds the camera steady for longer exposures.

2. Composition. Photographing subjects in groups of three covers them best. Overall orientation photographs show the big picture, intermediates show the subject of attention in its immediate surroundings, and the close up shot shows the evidence in detail. The photographer includes orientation arrows and rulers for scale. Investigators have many subscenes to photograph for a thorough treatment of a private scene. A thorough complement of photographs includes multiple shots from different perspectives. The investigator uses orientation arrows and rulers for scale to show details in perspective.

The composition quality considers the art of how the photographer sets up the image from a perspective, and what he includes in the images. This includes taking images of the same subject from three different distances to show context and evidence. The overall shot shows the big picture, like an entire room. The intermediate shot shows a small area surrounding a specific target subject, such as a bureau top with a jewelry box. A close up shot shows details like a fingerprint on top of the jewelry box with orientation arrows and scales to clarify sizes. The photographer takes photographs with and without the scales and measuring tape to avoid the appearance of hiding evidence.

Hosting scene photographs can rely on natural lighting when places like unimproved areas lack electric service. The investigator overcomes this with equipment including a good camera, portable lighting, and a good flash. Public scenes work well for video based scene photographic documentation when the scenes take up larger areas, and video allows the investigator some latitude about the exact borders and barriers to the scene.

Most investigators remove drugs from a person before taking photographs of them as found. Body cameras help remedy this common problem for investigators. Drug photographs show the drug's appearance along with the packaging.

Scenes require a number of shots to cover the evidence. The four types of approaches include hosting scenes, cars, tools, and persons.

a. Private and public scenes.

1. Eight compass perspectives on the subject of the image.

2. The outside looking in.

3. The barriers to entry, and potential entries, locks, and security.

4. The entry point.

5. The transit routes from the entry point.

6. Controls including lights, door knobs, and all others.

7. The center of gravity or focus of the crime.

8. Close ups of any evidence, or damage.

9. The inside looking out.

10. The exit point.

11. Spaces with roofs still benefit from overhead images to show how the scene works. Firetrucks provide an overhead view, but some investigators rely on drones.

12. Some investigators photograph the gathered crowd of onlookers to later use. This only proves presence at a scene after a crime, but as a longshot it could pay off

b. Car Scenes.

1. Eight compass perspectives on the subject of the image.

2. The view of the outside from inside, such as through the front windshield.

3. The barriers to entry, and potential entries, locks, and security.

4. The entry point.

5. The license plate and VIN.

6. The various zones inside including the center of gravity and the

7. Overhead and sometimes the undercarriage.

8. The trunk.

9. The engine compartment.

10. The passenger compartment.

11. Close ups of any evidence, or damage.

c. Tool Scenes.

1. The hosting scene.

2. Eight points around the tool.

3. The serial number, make and model, caliber if relevant.

4. The interior of the tool such as a gun's chamber.

5. Files or screenshots showing what the device holds

6. Close ups of interaction point, any evidence, identifying features, or damage.

7. Any associated equipment like a magazine, and spare ammunition.

8. The serial number, make and model.

d. Person Scenes

1. The hosting scene where the person spent time.

2. Eight compass perspectives, and the top. A varied selection aids in matching with other images where the person stood at various angles.

3. Photographs of persons in various stages of undress when it has a crime based reason. A person scene's three layers require the investigator collect photographs of at least a person's covering layer, and exterior. A person's interior layer photographs such as x-rays for bone or dental structure can have relevance for identification.

4. The common interaction points including the head, face, hands, feet, sex organs, tattoos, birthmarks, and any identifying feature.

5. Close ups of any evidence, or damage.

C. Preserve. Photography requires a computer for processing and storage. Some departments have dedicated servers with limited connections to ensure the images remain pure. High-capacity memory encourages taking more photographs.

D. Process. Computers automate digital photography processing. The camera saves images on a memory device, which the investigator transfers to a hard drive or server. The photographer can enhance and reduce features of the image with software. Digital photography has eliminated the chemical development of photographs associated with digital prints. Sometimes an investigator may need an image enhanced, and eliminate what clouds the image to access the key parts.

1. Refine. Software can also help make the image usable in ways like adjusting the colors in shadows.

2. Standardize. Scales allow the investigator to standardize the sizes in an image. Standardization allows for comparisons and matching for patterns and fingerprints.

3. Interpret. Investigators can interpret the subject of images such as in identifying persons, and also what the image shows.

E. Technical Admissibility. Judges consider if the images provide a true and accurate representation of their subject. Attorneys call to question the science of the photo in accordance with Daubert and Frye if the photographer used specialized processes and equipment to obtain the images, such as chemicals to make features visible or light wavelength enhancement. Filters may enhance certain features in a scene, and the investigator may receive questions about the science behind the altered images. If a filter makes bruising visible, science must validate the process.

F. Legal Admissibility. Judges consider if the investigator who took the photo violated a person's rights by collecting the images. This includes images citizens or infrastructure captured, as well as images the investigator captured.

II. Evidence Analysis

A. Cause. Photographic evidence comes into existence as the effect from all five major causes: intentional, accidental, functional, habitual, and byproduct. The investigator takes photographs with intention.

B. Creation. Photographs reproduce what the lens sees, so the creation of photographic evidence documents the other evidence. A camera produces photographs as visual reproductions of the scenes within its view. The original evidence has its own creation path which the investigator looks at for its category from the other five evidence types. Sometimes the images represent the scene, and sometimes the images incorporate technology to accentuate certain features and reduce other in order to show evidence invisible to the naked eye such as biological fluids. The investigator photographs what she sees. Those photographic subjects come from construction, deconstruction, or transfer.

III. Evidence to Proof

A. Strengths. Photographic evidence provides a reproduction of situations, scenes, and evidence for a person to view instead of traveling to them. A picture shows how things looked at a particular moment. A picture can show what it takes thousands of words to express, and can include the evidence to prove facts. Photography does not alter the subject of the image, so the investigator can work on any evidence type after without interference. Citizen precrime photographs show the scene before the effects of the interactions. Investigators take most official photographs after the crime to show the outcome. Photographs carry identification evidence if the photo shows enough of a person for someone to identify him. Investigator photographs also aid in finding physical evidence like citizen photographs do, and the investigator may realize the significance of items in a photograph after processing the scene.

1. Accuracy. Investigator photographs have opportunities for accurate portrayals of evidence when the investigator has the time to set up the shot, and control the elements like lighting. Photographs capture how scenes looked at a specific time and location. Photographs document the scenes, and decisions taken during investigations, such as how a scene looked, before, during, and at the conclusion of an investigation. The investigator combines multiple images to show a progression, such as the life cycle of a bruise. Sometimes an investigator finds hidden evidence after removing the top layer. Photographs show levels of evidence, and progress as the investigator removes evidence. Photographs provide portable replacement evidence to show the scene. Sometimes the investigator leaves the original evidence such as the bruised flesh on a victim, or damaged buildings. The camera's focus and lighting showing the details impacts the level of precision for photographs. Cameras embed a timestamp in the photographic files when they capture an image. Some have GPS built in to provide the location useful for the order of shots within the collection, called geotagging. These features benefit investigators when citizens provide photographic evidence.

2. Uniqueness. The investigator also has the opportunity to show each evidence item she photographs for its uniqueness. Magnification clarifies uniqueness.

3. Proof Ability. Photographs by the investigator can prove facts in a two dimensional way.

B. Weaknesses. A photograph's strength of showing how things look also can serve as a weakness when a camera gives an appearance and not always facts. Camera devices still lack the range, precision, and adjustment of the human eye in seeing objects under many conditions. Images only appeal to a person's sense of sight, depriving the observer of all other senses, such as weight, smell, taste, temperature, and texture. While cameras capture scenes, they can only show what they see.

1. Vulnerability. A photographer's ability to collect and retain an image determines its vulnerability. Photographic evidence has little vulnerability to time in the digital realm. System failures happen, and so do technology changes, but images do not fade as they did when printed on paper.

a. Environment. The investigator must have access to the scene to photograph it. Weather may impact photography. In order to collect photographic evidence, the camera must capture the subject at the right time. Everything changes with time. Some of the investigator's best photographs come early in the investigation before scenes alter. Digital photographs require software and computers to maintain and preserve them, making them as vulnerable as any data system.

b. Person. Investigators can still take bad images with automated cameras if they have a poor sense of composition. They can forget to take photographs at any time in the process.

2. Countermeasures. A person can engage countermeasures for photographs a lot like he could with measurements by moving things within a scene.

3. Proof Inability. The investigator can only photograph the scene in front of her, and only the surface. The photograph serves to show how things looked at a particular time, often long after the crime.

C. Evidence Strengthening. Photographs providing visual evidence appeal to some juries more than words in statements, but may only stand in for physical evidence.

1. Documentary. . Images can show physical and documentary evidence in both direct and indirect forms. Photographic evidence pairs with all other evidence types as documentary evidence like information. Photographs need contextual information to set the stage for what they show.

2. Corroboration. Photographs support all other evidence processes and outcomes. Whatever the investigator photographs, having the original can aid the case.

3.2.2 WORKING CITIZEN PHOTOGRAPHS

The investigator uses citizen photographs to memorialize details of the case before the investigator got involved.

Goal. The investigator seeks to observe details about scenes and evidence by looking at citizen or non-investigator generated images to use as stand-alone or contributing facts in the case.

I. Evidence Collection

A. Find. Photographs also come from cameras controlled by infrastructure or citizens. The equipment can have similarities with the investigator's kit, but the investigator must obtain the images from the person in control of them.

1. Persons. The investigator may obtain photographs from persons who control the means of their production, such as when a person takes cellphone photographs, or has a security system. Photographs from a citizen, such as suspect, victim, or witness can show the action or other stages in the crime like preparation or recovery. The investigator often trades image quality for what it can prove.

2. Places. Photographs from infrastructure come from a camera in a scene, attached to the scene. Security systems may have fixed fields of vision, or have a movable system, like with retail security cameras. A smartphone's camera can act as infrastructure.

3. Things. Some things have cameras like phones, or like places.

B. Extract. The investigator obtains the images taken by citizens.

1. Technical. The investigator's skill centers on transferring the image from the hosting device to a department device. Citizen photographs come from built in security systems and smartphones.

2. Composition. Security system and smartphone photographs vary in composition. Security systems may capture action at strategic location, and provide movie style documentation. Smartphones may capture single shots or video also.

C. Preserve. The investigator collects citizen photographs by taking the already captured shots from the device.

D. Process. The investigator processes citizen images the same way as investigator images. He can use software tool to clarify the details the same ways as with his own images to refine, standardize, and interpret.

E. Technical Admissibility. Courts look at citizen images the same way as with investigator images. They ensure the photographer captured them and the investigator processed them by acceptable scientific procedure.

F. Legal Admissibility. Courts consider if the investigator obtained the photographs by violating a person's rights.

II. Evidence Analysis

A. Cause. Citizen photographic evidence comes into existence as the effect from all five major causes: intentional, accidental, functional, habitual, and byproduct. The infrastructure cameras takes photographs with intention, but capture everything, even the unintended. Citizens including suspects, victims, and witnesses, take photographs with smartphones by intention. Sometimes persons intend to the take them as entertainment, only to have them later used as evidence.

B. Creation. Cameras work the same as they do for investigators and capture the scene in two dimensions at a particular moment in time. The scenes can result from construction, deconstruction, or transfer of evidence.

III. Evidence to Proof

A. Strengths. Citizen photographic evidence has the potential strength of timeliness and centrality. Citizen photographs can provide key evidence at specific times in the crime. Investigators and juries alike appreciate seeing what happened more than hearing about it.

1. Accuracy. Citizen photographs may capture the moment of the crime, defining details of identification and action.

2. Uniqueness. Citizen photographs can offer views of how things looked before and during the crime, unique conditions often changed during the course of events.

3. Proof Ability. Citizen images can also provide proof showing who did what.

B. Weaknesses. Citizen photographs often reflect limitations of image quality, equipment, and photographer ability.

1. Vulnerability. Citizen images have all the vulnerabilities of investigator images, and they may not have tech support to ensure quality.

2. Countermeasures. Suspects may use countermeasures against security cameras such as covering the lens or even wearing disguises. Suspects with total control of hosting scenes and the persons within may take smartphones from persons who photograph them.

3. Proof Inability. Citizen photographs can only capture the scene as it was. The citizen or system taking the shot has the same limitations as the investigator.

C. Evidence Strengthening. Citizen images offer strong evidence which the investigator may enhance.

1. Documentary. Whoever took the images often can make a statement documenting how, and what the images show. If the images come from a suspect, the investigator must including how she obtained the pictures.

2. Corroboration. The investigator strengthens images by providing related evidence. Investigator images validating the same scenes, evidence, and sometimes dynamics bolster the citizen images.

3.3 WORKING ARTIFACTS

Artifacts stand alone as portable evidence or scenes with their associated evidence. Artifacts have two types:

3.3.1 Object Artifacts

3.3.2 Trace Artifacts

Goal. The investigator seeks artifacts as evidence to show scene interaction and a shift of control in an investigation.

3.3.1 WORKING OBJECT ARTIFACTS

Objects act as self-contained scenes made into evidence by a controlling person as a scene within a scene.

Goal. The investigator seeks to collect object artifacts to prove a transfer of control and to prove who did what.

I. Evidence Collection

A. Find. The investigator collects artifacts from the size of jewels and larger from all scenes.

1. Persons. The investigator finds person scene artifacts when he has access to the person. Persons have artifacts near their interaction points, while avoiding interfering with them. A person has jewelry around the neck, wrists, and ankles. His pockets contain valuables, and items relevant to his activities.

2. Places. Investigators can find stored or discarded artifacts in place scenes. Artifacts may not appear out of place given scenes contain large amounts of evidence.

3. Things. Artifacts connected with other artifacts can take the form of ancillary equipment, such as a case or computer peripheral.

B. Extract. The investigator finds and collects artifacts without damage. If the evidence has a lower threshold of technical expertise and equipment, the investigator does it himself. Scenes host artifact evidence, providing a contextual significance by its role as an object manipulated, controlled, or possessed by at least one person in a crime. Most artifacts large enough to see preexist the crime. They include things showing a transfer of control like items of value or weapons. The investigator locates bigger artifacts with ease when he had context or a statement from an involved person to identify it. Their discovery locations may relate more to storage than to control or action, and persons may discard objects without intention. Artifacts may appear out of place, like a wallet in a park. The investigator treats artifacts as their own self-contained scene, collecting them only after documenting their exact locations and situation, photographing them in place, and isolating them in sealed packages to prevent evidence getting into or out of the packaging.

C. Preserve. Sealing evidence artifacts at the hosting scene reduces chances of contamination. Some equipment remains in the lab so the investigator may have to open the seal for processing later or forward the artifact to other facilities like laboratories for processing for evidence. Evidence artifacts should not leave the secure hosting unsealed, as it invites contamination. The investigator stores larger objects in boxes, sealed with tape, or unused paint cans. Bloody or wet clothing requires a drier to prevent rotting.

D. Process. Some artifacts require more processing than others given their uniqueness, identifiability, and role in a case. Object artifacts may act as self-contained scenes with a full complement of evidence. Artifacts may need an expert opinion on their features, and uses. Even mundane artifacts can require a technician such as a lab worker to identify drug types.

a. Refine. Artifacts can require little refinement beyond the evidence connected with them or they may act as the key to the case with many facets.

b. Standardize. Factory production makes artifact similar, but the investigator or technician can choose features present in multiple objects to differentiate each one providing a unique identification for each piece.

c. Interpret. Many times artifacts require little interpretation. They arrive as direct evidence of facts. An artifact belonging to one person in the possession of another without authorization needs as little interpretation as a gun in the possession of someone alleged to have committed a robbery.

E. Technical Admissibility. An artifact's technical admissibility comes from the investigator's methods of finding and collecting the item. Artifacts themselves need little processing, but the evidence on or in them requires the standard processes like other scenes.

F. Legal Admissibility. Judges consider if the investigator had the right to search and seize the artifact as a part of the case.

II. Evidence Analysis

A. Cause. Artifact evidence comes into existence as the effect from all causes: intentional, accidental, functional, habitual, and byproduct.

1. Intentional. Some persons control an artifact, bringing it into the case like a weapon.

2. Accidental. When the interactions of scenes results in unintended evidence, like a suspect leaving a smartphone in a hosting scene they create accidental evidence.

3. Functional. When the interaction of scenes achieves something, the interaction creates functional evidence like a stabbing creates blood, or prying a door creates paint chips and tool marks.

4. Habitual. When a person performs tasks as he always does, he creates evidence out of habit. A suspect who takes his phone out of his pocket when he gets home may do the same thing in a crime scene.

5. Byproduct. When the interactions of scenes create evidence related to the crime, but not at the center of the crime, like a robbery suspect who pockets an ATM receipt after using a stolen access card.

B. Creation. Artifacts include tools to assist someone in doing or fighting a crime, and objects of crimes.

A. Synthesis. Artifacts come as self-contained scenes. How the investigator finds them provides some indication of their creation. Evidence artifacts synthesize by construction, deconstruction, or transfer.

1. Construction. Artifact evidence constructs when multiple entities or situations come together to make a new scene. Two legal chemicals combined to make a bomb constitute the construction of evidence. The chemicals may present as trace.

2. Deconstruction. Most deconstruction creates trace evidence unless the parts' size makes them objects like a broken hammer head.

3. Transfer. Evidence artifacts' origin may lie near or far from the crime and many crimes involve transference of artifacts in terms of location and control. For example, a victim's TV synthesized into evidence when the suspect touched it as part of a crime dynamic. The suspect removed the TV, and transferred it to her home where an investigator discovered it.

III. Evidence to Proof

A. Strengths. Artifacts show identification, presence, actions, control and possession, but they make up the first set of evidence in its pure form. Artifact evidence provides high strength proof if the evidence has a unique identity. Persons obtain them as the fruits of the crime, which show a change of control. A person who touched an artifact, had presence or control of it, a major component of law. Evidence artifacts can identify by association as a bridge between a person and another scene.

1. Accuracy. Artifact evidence's nearness to the actual facts relates to its accuracy as direct evidence and indirect evidence, also known as circumstantial evidence. The investigator can define each evidence artifact with accuracy by its uniqueness. A person may involve an artifact in a case as a peripheral object which could only show presence. A central object could show presence as well as action, control and impact as an accurate set of facts.

Investigators make cases by finding the uniqueness about the evidence in order to make it specific. Stating the evidence proves suspect wore shoes does not do a lot for the case, but proving the suspect wore a particular size, color, and model shoe with specific defects and marks distinguishes the shoe as an artifact among all other shoes in the world.

2. Uniqueness. Each artifact has unique features, but an investigator identifies the unique features making the artifact identifiable. Magnification reveals documentable and objective differences. Artifacts scale down to microscopic size. Serialized items overcome the uniformity problems of mass production of similar items.

3. Proof Ability. Artifact quality pivots on its uniqueness. A serialized or personalized artifact or one carrying identifying evidence provides higher quality proof than evidence without the uniqueness. The investigator has to prove double interactions of artifact evidence to get to useful facts of cause and effect. The interactions include artifact to person, artifact to hosting scene, and artifact to any other scene. The evidence proves presence and action without identification of a person connected with the item.

B. Weaknesses. An artifact's weaknesses center on the investigator's inability to recognize their significance, and failure to distinguish them. Unrecognized evidence does not make it into the case, and has no ability to prove any facts. Non-unique evidence artifacts prove little in the case. Evidence artifacts provide little in the way of a timeline other than relative times. The lack of databases limits the investigator's ability to match stolen property. Most agencies run databases only cross referencing with pawn shops to show temporary ownership. The laws and databases have not caught up with the massive stolen goods market on the internet using websites to sell ill-gotten items. Portability and provable uniqueness limit artifact evidence capabilities of identification, presence, action, or damage.

1. Vulnerability. Each piece of evidence has its own vulnerabilities damaging its reliability. The more time an artifact goes uncollected, the greater the danger an event might damage its value to proving facts. Artifacts hold up well over time, even if the evidence included with them does not.

a. Environment. The weather surrounding the evidence artifact makes it vulnerable to alteration or destruction, as well as follow on transfer.

b. Person. Persons might manipulate the artifact prior to photographing or collecting it.

2. Countermeasures. Suspects control object artifacts during their crimes, and continue to try to control them as countermeasures. Destroying, altering or tainting artifacts with matter can reduce their usefulness in proving a case, but only taking the artifact from the hosting scene can prevent its use by the investigator.

3. Proof Inability. Object artifacts cannot prove identification by direct means. Finding a suspect's wallet in a crime scene points the case in a direction, but does not prove he brought it into the scene during crime all by itself.

C. Reinforcing Evidence. Artifact objects make up one of the oldest forms of evidence, and require minimal reinforcement.

1. Documentary. Artifact evidence require context of information and sometimes photographs. Documentary evidence creates context.

2. Corroboration. Citizen photographs of objects in different scenes can help corroborate facts about object artifacts. Identifying evidence of biological evidence, and fingerprints on object artifacts can provide the means to determine who controlled the evidence. Only dental patterns among patterns can identify persons' interaction with object artifacts.

3.3.2 WORKING TRACE ARTIFACTS

Trace evidence such as dust, fluids, or gases act as artifacts with small size, acting as a scene within a scene, shifting from one scene to another.

Goal. The investigator seeks to collect trace artifacts to prove an interaction, and sometimes a transfer of control.

I. Evidence Collection

A. Find. The investigator collects smaller artifacts in all the places as object artifacts, but sometimes in less obvious places. Trace can come from inanimate scenes, or include biological material.

1. Persons. Investigators locate living (DNA) and nonliving trace. Trace containing biological evidence relates to person's body castoffs. Persons often have trace near and on top of their interaction points.

2. Places. Investigators can find trace artifacts in scenes at interaction points or along pathways where the person travelled.

3. Things. Artifacts hold trace such as dust, or biological matter. Smaller artifacts like trace such as dirt may require close attention to pathways, or interaction points requiring force to dislodge the trace from one scene to another. Tiny evidence comes from small material which flaked off one scene, ending up in another. Trace comes without intention.

B. Extract. Collecting trace evidence requires a way to locate it, and save it. The ALS can help visualize the material. Small evidence articles like dust, chemicals, or hair come from interactions during the crime leading to their construction or deconstruction. Smaller evidence from deconstruction requires the investigator find the area where the evidence deconstructed. This requires more skill with hard to see evidence. The investigator uses equipment to find artifacts ranging from simple magnifying lenses to tape for lifting. The investigator also has to collect the evidence in a way to ensure its preservation after documenting their exact locations and situation, photographing them in place, and isolating them in sealed packages to prevent evidence getting into or out of the packaging. GSR comes with its own collection kits, and the investigator sends the kits to a lab for chemical pattern matching.

C. Preserve. Sealing evidence artifacts at the hosting scene reduces chances of contamination. Tape lifts collect dust and small matter. Some investigators collect material in a bindle, plastic bag, or glass jar.

D. Process. The investigator requires a laboratory to process the trace even though they act as their own tiny crime scenes. A technician uses microscopes to examine the trace for matching properties. A technician also may test the trace with chemicals to see if their compositions match.

a. Refine. Smaller material can get lost among other matter, so the technician often has to parse out the relevant material.

b. Standardize. A technician or expert standardizes trace artifacts by identification.

c. Interpret. Trace artifacts connect scenes when an expert identifies the matter as connected to another sample.

E. Technical Admissibility. Obtaining and processing trace artifacts require more documentation to show the investigator obtained the evidence in a scientific manner acceptable by Daubert or Frye standards. Technical admissibility covers more of the processing as it brings out the evidentiary qualities in the matter. Opposing attorneys cross examine the processes for errors.

F. Legal Admissibility. Courts consider if the investigator had the right to search and seize the trace artifacts as a part of the case.

II. Evidence Analysis

A. Cause. Trace artifact evidence often comes about from the deconstruction of a scene as the byproduct of an interaction. Car crashes cause a paint transfer.

B. Creation. Most trace artifact evidence has its origins in deconstruction of scenes. Trace often consists of material chipped or flaked from a larger scene, such as paint chips from a crashed car.

III. Evidence to Proof

A. Strengths. Trace artifact evidence can prove presence and action with its matching material if available.

1. Accuracy. Trace evidence's specific formula increase its accuracy.

2. Uniqueness. Trace evidence can connect two scenes together by the uniqueness of the material. Biological trace evidence may connect with a particular person.

3. Proof Ability. Trace evidence shows a material source, and can indicate dynamics for the formulation of evidence, such as wood flakes from prying a door open.

B. Weaknesses. Independent identification without something to compare the trace evidence with can challenge laboratories and technicians. Trace evidence may not have enough uniqueness for positive identification on its own.

1. Vulnerability. Each piece of evidence has its own vulnerabilities damaging its reliability. The more time an artifact goes uncollected, the greater the danger an event might damage its value to proving facts. Trace artifacts often hold up well over time.

a. Environment. The investigator can miss small trace artifact evidence in a scene. Small size also makes the evidence light enough for wind to carry it away or destroy it in place.

b. Person. A person can easily bring about weather like conditions and blow the evidence away, or mistake the trace for a mess and clean it up.

2. Countermeasures. Suspects can destroy trace evidence by dispersing it, or tainting it with the addition of other trace.

3. Proof Inability. Trace artifacts cannot prove a person's identity by themselves given they do not carry biological material or fingerprints.

D. Companion Evidence. Artifact evidence require context of information and sometimes photographs. Artifact evidence's companion evidence includes all evidence. Documentary evidence creates context. Identifying evidence of biological evidence, and fingerprints provide the means to determine who controlled the evidence.

C. Reinforcing Evidence. The investigator can reinforce trace evidence the same ways as with evidence artifacts

1. Documentary. The investigator's recording of evidence processes bolster the evidence by documenting its history. Trace often involves more processing to magnify the material for documentation and comparison.

2. Corroboration. Trace evidence artifact evidence transfers by deconstruction or division, so other evidence showing a connection between scenes can corroborate the connection proved by trace. Additional evidence supporting the same scene connection can corroborate facts from proof.

3.4 WORKING BIOLOGICAL MATERIAL

Biological material has components for investigators to use to solve cases by identification. Biological material evidence comes in two types:

3.4.1 Serology

3.4.2 DNA

Goal. The investigator seeks biological evidence to show scene interactions and identification in an investigation.

3.4.1 WORKING SEROLOGY

Investigators use serology to identify and classify biological material resembling trace evidence from a person's body scene to support the investigation by indicating what part of a person interacted with another scene.

Goal. The investigator seeks to collect biological material and process it for serological evidence to prove what part of the body produced the material.

I. Evidence Collection

A. Find. Serology helps identify the body part where the biological material came from. The body part or area has significance in many cases by indicating activity related to a person's part of the body. Semen implies different activity than saliva. The study of serology covers body fluids including blood, saliva, sweat (perspiration), breast milk, vomit, urine, feces, semen, vaginal fluid, and mucous. The investigator often deals with additional material such as fingernails, hair, and cells. Each part of serology has tests for the investigator in the field to presumptively identify the material. This also validates the material as biological, paving the way for DNA testing.

1. Persons. Parts of the human body produce specific purpose biological material. Each of these types of evidence provides insight into events, like presence and dynamics. The serological evidence from a person can end up on a person in the same areas it comes from another. The body collects and carries the biological evidence anywhere, but interaction points on person scenes represent the high value target areas.

a. Hair. Hair falls off persons in the natural course of events, but persons may pull it out during a fight. The evidence arrives to another scene either by direct path, such as through contact or by discarding and conditions such as wind when blood drops on the floor.

b. Saliva. A person's saliva has skin cells sloughed off from the cheek and indicate the person placed his mouth on a scene, or spat. Persons deposit saliva anywhere on another person's body.

c. Skin. A person's skin cells slough off everywhere on the body, and a person can transfer cells from body to body.

d. Semen and vaginal fluid. Persons have semen and vaginal fluid contain cells traveling with these fluids. Semen implies sexual arousal, or intimacy. Vaginal fluid may indicate arousal, or intimacy. These fluids may travel to another person's face, hands, or genitalia.

e. Blood cells. White blood cells carry a nucleus while red blood cells lose their nucleus and can indicate a wound on a person opened the flow. Persons bleed on each other, such as after a fight, and the blood can land on the hands, shoes, or anywhere else.

f. Sweat. A person's sweat carries skin cells with it as it travels. Persons can sweat in lower temperatures, and if intimate share the perspiration with other persons.

g. Urine. A technician can identify what the person had inside by what his urine or dried stain contains.

h. Feces. Persons also rarely defecate on other persons, but like urination, it can happen on most areas of the body.

Biological material travels, has secondary transfer capabilities, and endures rough conditions. Wind blows the material from another location.

2. Places. Persons deposit biological evidence on places by touch and spillage. Interaction points represent the higher opportunity to obtain biological evidence, but spillage means the investigator may locate evidence without a direct connection between source and discovery points. Persons donate biological material everywhere they interact.

3. Things. Investigators find things or artifacts have biological evidence connections based more on direct interaction, and less on spillage. So while a person may slough off skin cells while in a car, and they land on a head rest without touch, a person who touches a gun leaves cells on the artifact.

B. Extract. Collecting biological material in or on crime scenes requires the investigator to find the evidence, and decide its value to the case. Hosting scenes often bring the greatest challenge with this with their larger spaces, and higher population of potential donors within them. The evidence collection processes alter the scene, but the investigator still collects fingerprints and patterns marks after DNA without contamination.

The investigator wears PPE to prevent cross contamination of evidence during collection. The ALS can help visualize the material. Testing kits can identify the type of material. The investigator collects the biological material with new sterile swabs, and uses sterile water to help collect dry stains. The material's endurance challenges the investigator to obtain context and relevance with the evidence. An investigator's techniques synchronize with the laboratory technician's requirements.

C. Preserve. Most biological material requires a cold environment to stop the constant changes in living things. Moisture compounds the problem, and a lot of materials have a liquid component. Most labs refrigerate samples like blood or urine draws.

D. Process. The investigator may use field serology tests to determine if a material has origins from a part of a body. Presumptive tests can identify where on the body the material came from such as saliva, seminal fluid, vaginal fluid, or blood. A laboratory may confirm the serology tests. Most investigators identify blood or semen in an early phase relying on ALS equipment and chemical testing like Phenolphthalein to test for blood and provide definitive identification. Investigators and technicians still use many tests predating DNA for their ability to identify biological material by its source from the body.

a. Refine. Clean and pure samples help allow the technician to seek the chemicals defining the biological material.

b. Standardize. Each type of biological material has its own chemical formula which the technician can identify.

c. Interpret. Identifying the origin of the biological material can help define the actions of the person who provided the material.

E. Technical Admissibility. Biological evidence collection and sequencing has many steps with science. Most serology tests have passed the tests for reliability in both Daubert and Frye, but the courts still review the evidence to make certain the investigators obtained it in accordance with guidelines.

F. Legal Admissibility. Attorneys and judges evaluate the collection and sequencing of material for its adherence to laws protecting citizen's rights to privacy.

II. Evidence Analysis

A. Cause. Every piece of evidence comes into existence as the effect from some cause. When the investigator can determine the cause behind the evidence it moves the case closer to solving. Most biological evidence comes as a result of a body function, either by intention or accident such as semen from sexual arousal, or bleeding from a stabbing.

B. Creation. Biological evidence comes from a person ready to transfer after the person constructs it or deconstructs it from his person and transfers it. Biological evidence creation happens within an organism like a person, and transfers from the person to another scene. The investigator may discover the serological evidence at the synthesis site, or at a different location. For example, a suspect rapes a victim and ejaculates in her vagina. The biological evidence originates from the suspect. The victim's vagina is the synthesis site. The victim showers before the investigator has the opportunity to send her for a medical exam. She discarded her underwear in the hamper. Her underwear is the discovery site of the suspect's biological material. The victim's vaginal fluid could also go from her body to the suspect's penis, and end up on the suspect's underwear which he discarded in his hamper. In both cases the underwear carries the serological evidence of both persons, indicating body part origins, and DNA to identify the persons (covered in the next section).

III. Evidence to Proof

A. Strengths. Serological biological evidence provides a basic identification of where on a body the material came from, indicating possible activities.

1. Accuracy. The specific identification of the source of biological material provides specific information about scene interaction. This accuracy defines what interacted.

2. Uniqueness. Specific body origins for material narrow the possibilities of action between scenes.

3. Proof Ability. Proving the origin on a body of the biological material evidence helps define the actions as they fit within crimes.

B. Weaknesses. Serological evidence (excluding DNA) does not identify a person, and narrows the investigation without defining a suspect. Before DNA technician used blood typing to narrow down the suspect pool, and clear the innocent who had a different blood type.

1. Vulnerability. Biological evidence has the highest vulnerability of all the evidence types covered. Living things can decay faster than non-living things but some biological lasts a long time. Absent the second two factors of vulnerability, rotting soft tissue may last only a few days, while bones last hundreds or thousands of years.

a. Environment. Biological evidence degrades in the elements. The material may rot in place, or migrate from the initial site of the interaction. While biological evidence and DNA hold up well over time in the right conditions of a sealed environment away from destructive forces, material left unsecured has higher vulnerability.

b. Person. A person moves or destroys the evidence without effort or intent. Persons cross contaminate DNA evidence by introducing DNA and biological material into samples. Investigators without adequate safeguards against cross contamination have ruined samples and compromised cases. If the investigator had contact with both the suspect and victim scenes, the evidence has the potential for cross contamination which the investigator must explain.

2. Countermeasures. Suspects often try to clean the scene to remove traces of biological evidence like blood. Washing the surfaces with bleach only dilutes the material, and enough blood remain to cause a reaction with the serological tests.

3. Proof Inability. Serology on its own does not identify persons until the lab analyzes the DNA.

B. Weaknesses. Evidence provides detailed or limited facts of identification, presence, action, control, and damage, but while biological evidence can indicate activity by the origin of the material from a body, it can arrive to a scene by unintentional ways making for less clear interpretations.

C. Reinforcing Evidence. The investigator shores up serological biological evidence by providing detailed information about it, and including related evidence.

1. Documentary. Biological evidence for serology requires information as context, and photographs as documentation.

2. Corroboration. Biological evidence for serology may find corroboration with image evidence showing activity supporting the biological evidence.

3.4.2 WORKING DNA

Investigators use DNA from biological material to identify specific persons and support the investigation.

Goal. The investigator seeks to collect biological material and process it for DNA evidence to prove who provided the sample.

I. Evidence Collection

A. Find. Nuclear DNA (Deoxyribonucleic Acid) serves as identifying biological evidence from a person. Most scenes hold DNA, but only person scenes (and all animal scene analogs) create DNA and distribute it with biological material such as skin cells, hair, body fluids, and fingernails.

B. Extract. The investigator finds and collects DNA in the same manner as other biological material for serology.

C. Preserve. Labs freeze most DNA swabs, and most evidence articles with biological material components like bloody clothing. However, metal with biological material does not freeze well, and labs store them at room temperature in sealed paper boxes to retain the connected biological evidence.

D. Process. The collection of biological material requires using sterile packaging material, and taking personal precautions to avoid contaminating the sample. A laboratory may confirm the serology tests, and will sequence the DNA. Sometimes the investigator has no need to test for serology and can go direct to DNA. Technicians have obtained DNA from hats with no reason to determine where on the suspect's person the DNA came from.

Expert technicians identify the source of biological material using complex equipment and biostatistics. DNA's expense lies in testing costs dwarfing most other testing costs. Most departments regulate its use to person crimes and department policies may eliminate testing a viable sample based on the crime type. With no other identifying evidence crimes go unsolved.

a. Refine. Labs avoid sequencing DNA from blind swabs collected from the exterior of a car after a burglary. A technician cannot connect the sample to the person who broke in, and touching the exterior falls short of proving a break in. Labs sequence samples from cases where a person touched a car's exterior, such as a hit and run, where the investigation provides contextual information about the sample relating it to the crime event. Degraded samples provide some value, as the biostatistician or technician provides some statistical insight into the odds of a match.

b. Standardize. The DNA testing looks at the same loci regardless of the cell's origin. Technicians sequence the DNA in order to decode it and obtain the specific information used to identify persons. Once the scientists identify each locus, they upload the data to databases. The FBI maintains the Combined DNA Index System, (CODIS). State and county databases provide faster searching but with limited localized coverage. Private labs sequence customers DNA for law enforcement on contract, as well as commercial use including healthcare predictions.

c. Interpret. Technicians intertwine statistics with biology for crime fighting DNA. The laboratory provides three possible results, a non-match, inconclusive, or a match. The statistical component of DNA becomes more important as investigators rely more on familial DNA matching. Biostatisticians take an unknown DNA profile and calculate potential family members. They use the group of profiles to search DNA profiles in CODIS or in private sequencers to see if they identify a family member. Investigators determine how close the known DNA profile relates to the unknown profile by degrees, and develop a suspect to the point of obtaining a sample of his DNA to sequence and compare. Persons who have the same father, but different mothers have recognizable statistical features, as do fathers of their children, and other blood relations.

Most cases involve at least two rounds of sequencing of samples. The investigator submits a sample collected from the scene, and a potential match, or suspect. If technician connect a suspect to the case, they repeat the testing to ensure accuracy. A person transfers DNA to another person, necessitating three sequencings: the suspect, the victim, and the sample of material from one or the other persons.

E. Technical Admissibility. Biological evidence collection and sequencing has many steps with science. DNA has passed the tests for reliability in both Daubert and Frye, but the courts still review the evidence to make certain the investigators obtained it in accordance with guidelines.

F. Legal Admissibility. Attorneys and judges evaluate the collection and sequencing of DNA for its adherence to laws protecting citizen's rights to privacy.

II. Evidence Analysis

A. Cause. Biological material has both serology and DNA as study areas. The causes of DNA are the same as the causes of serology.

B. Creation. Biological evidence including DNA comes off a person ready to transfer. A person's cells construct the DNA within the cell, and the material can break off and deconstruct from the greater body as part of the transfer process. Most DNA collection from suspects involve the investigator swabbing a person's mouth for their cheeks cells (buccal) which have a high production an shed rate.

1. Construction. Persons and other living things construct biological evidence and DNA in the cell production process. The body makes evidence when it makes cells. If two persons conceive a child then both contribute DNA to the child. Pregnancy provides strong evidence two people had sexual intercourse. Most cases involve biological material of a single person, but biostatisticians can build a genetic family tree with DNA, determining parents, and other relatives.

Biological evidence and its core of DNA come from living things, but crime fighting biological material focuses on humans. Lifeforms produce DNA in the nucleus of cell as the instructions. Most criminal investigations focus on human DNA, but the science can identify other animals like dogs. All humans have over 99% similarity in DNA, and only a little less similarity with some primates. Lifeforms produce and discard DNA and biological material all the time. Persons lose skin cells, hair, and body fluids laden with cells. Person scenes alter scenes when they deposit their DNA onto other scenes. Technicians explain how quantities work to help guard against a false positive or secondary transfer. DNA and biological material withstands harsh environments. DNA survives in a place for a long time such as a mummy's tomb. Technicians have sequenced DNA subjected to fires with little degradation.

Person scenes have DNA in most cells. Nuclear DNA resides in the nucleus of the cell as a long string of compounds, represented by letters from its four letter alphabet A, T, C, and G. They pair up as G-C and A-T to form "words," and identify the 20 amino acids which make up proteins. These letters make up Short Tandem Repeats (STR), using the few options in a long chain of letters. A person's nuclear DNA contains around 6,000,000,000 letters. STR analysis looks at the patterns in those long chains.

A person has 23 chromosome pairs. The mother passes on 23, and the father passes on 23. The chromosomes come together to make the pairs. Within those pairs of chromosomes 20,000 to 25,000 genes make up the words, and letters. Each gene has a particular location (locus or loci for plural) on the chromosome with its own name. The alleles provide the information to specify the loci. The alleles at a locus make up a person's genotype. Each locus has its own number of possible alleles. Some loci have only a few allele options, while some have 20 or more.

Nuclear DNA testing sets the standard as the identification DNA, but technicians also conduct Mitochondrial DNA testing (MtDNA). Mitochondrial DNA comes from the mitochondria, the cellular organelles in eukaryotic cells. They change food into chemical energy for the cell. MtDNA passes through the mother with few changes providing usefulness in relating persons. MtDNA has around 17,000 base parts for only 37 base pairs.

Some genes control the development of a feature, such as eye color, or hair loss, while some genes' purpose still remains undetected. Some books refer to uncategorized genes as junk DNA almost like a placeholder, until science determines its purpose.

2. Deconstruction. Biological evidence comes by way of deconstruction, as the evidence separated from a person. Even though the person created the material or DNA independent of the crime and it deconstructed from the person independent of a crime act, the evidence results from deconstruction when a part of the person leaves the body and goes to another scene..

3. Transfer. Biological evidence transfers from the lifeform to another scene as covered in the transfer section on serology.

III. Evidence to Proof

A. Strengths. Biological evidence and DNA provide direct evidence of identification, and the type of material provides identification of the body part, which provides indirect evidence in the areas of proof ability: accuracy, facts, companion evidence, and strength. DNA evidence can identify most plants or animals. Microscopic DNA evidence coexists with DNA from other sources in scenes. DNA and biological evidence proves identity, presence, and sometimes action. Skin cells under someone's fingernails imply the person struggled with another person, while semen on clothing implies the person had a connection to sexual intercourse, or at least arousal. The facts prove presence if they stop short of proving what a person did.

1. Accuracy. Biological evidence and DNA has high precision as it can identify the material and its origin on the body, and the person (except for twins). Investigators have sought familial matches through commercial testing services marketing themselves as providing health insights and family medical information. These databases have helped solve many cases where the suspect never provided DNA, but a family member did. The investigator draws up a search warrant for a judge to sign specifying what profiles she wants to obtain. The investigator uses the results to support further investigation and obtain new samples from the suspect to test.

2. Uniqueness. Before January 1, 2017 the FBI's laboratory identified persons by looking at 13 loci or genes plus the sex gene. After January 1, 2017, the FBI looks at 20 core loci. The FBI requires at least eight loci to work with DNA for most cases. They accept fewer alleles for missing persons. Every person's normal DNA has those fields present. Each gene has its own number of possible combinations. DNA for investigation uses sequences a person's DNA, rendering the DNA to a code mathematical formula for each person, although identical twins have the same DNA. Technicians compare the codes to identify persons in a form of pattern recognition. The biostatistics of examining 13 genes (now increased to 20) out of

the 25,000 genes technicians identifies persons by statistics as one in around 400 trillion. The earth's population estimation of 8,000,000,000 fits into 400 trillion 50,000 times the total population of earth. DNA works with a statistical match, instead of an exact match. Using 20 loci expands the accuracy, and gives more options for making matches.

3. Proof Ability. The DNA component of biological evidence can prove the identity of the donor along with presence.

B. Weaknesses. Evidence provides detailed or limited facts of identification, presence, action, control, and damage, but while biological evidence can indicate activity by the origin of the material from a body, it can arrive to a scene by unintentional ways making for less clear interpretations. Databases for matching unknown suspects have far smaller coverage than fingerprint databases. Right now most investigations into unknown or unavailable suspects rely on the DNA database CODIS. The database limits the search parameters to arrestees for certain types of crimes for the criminal population. A person receiving a blood transfusion or organ transplant has multiple DNA sequences in his person. An artifact where the biological evidence resides provides indications about actions.

DNA's portability and spill ability create a weakness in its proof ability. The investigator addresses DNA's ability to travel to new scenes after its initial deposit on a scene. Other types of corroborating evidence shore up cases with portable DNA samples.

1. Vulnerability. DNA comes with the same vulnerabilities as serological biological evidence. Time, persons, and the environment all contribute to how fast the evidence disappears.

a. Environment. Warm, humid, windy environments destroy or move DNA.

b. Persons. Distinguishing between multiple donors in a sample challenges technicians and their equipment when a sample contains two or three donors. A door handle to a bank has dozens of different DNA profiles on it, overwhelming the system's ability to distinguish specific identifications.

2. Countermeasures. Biological material endures well in hostile environments. Suspects sometimes believe harsh chemical like bleach destroy the evidence and clean the scene with it. Suspect may also try to burn things. Those actions add more facts to the case.

3. Proof Inability. Technicians have no way to determine the age of DNA on its own. DNA evidence only establishes a relative timeline. While fingerprints obliterate prior prints with the latest touch, DNA coexists in various ages, with older DNA in the same place as new. DNA testing shows identical twins as the same identity as of 2019.

C. Reinforcing Evidence. DNA requires the investigator build evidence around

1. Documentary. Biological evidence and DNA receive attention as a miraculous

evidence solution to solve old and new cases. DNA evidence's significant limitations require a full complement of other evidence for the investigator to obtain the benefits. Documentary evidence provides context for the biological evidence. The history of the person scene who donated the DNA has relevance to identification.

2. Corroboration. DNA's strongest allies include the documentary evidence of information and photographs, but fingerprints can validate identification.

3.5 WORKING FINGERPRINTS

Fingerprints offer identifying evidence using the patterns from a person's finger-prints. Fingerprints come in three types:

3.5.1 Latent

3.5.2 Patent

3.5.3 Plastic

Goal. The investigator seeks fingerprint evidence to show scene interactions and identification limited to a person's hands in an investigation.

3.5.1 WORKING LATENT FINGERPRINTS

Investigators use latent fingerprints from invisible patterns (at first) to identify specific persons and support the investigation.

Goal. The investigator seeks to find and collect latent fingerprints to match with established records, identify the producing person, and determine specific actions involving a person touching the scene.

I. Evidence Collection

A. Find. Latent or invisible fingerprints present the most common type of fingerprints for the investigator to work. Their invisibility means the person making the prints cannot see how much evidence he makes. The investigator knows where to look and what tools to use to find the evidence. Investigators find usable prints when a scene accepts a fingerprint impression, and retains it. Fingerprints can only come from the hands of a person who touched another scene. The ALS can help visualize the material. Tuned lasers also produce light waves an investigator can use to see prints.

1. Persons. While persons create all fingerprints, few person scenes hold fingerprints. Most fingerprints on person scenes involve dead persons. Medical examiner personnel handle the processing as they have jurisdiction over dead bodies.

2. Places. Public scenes with the right surfaces yield fingerprints, and labs process any clear enough samples. Most fingerprint samples come from hard and smooth interaction points. Textured surfaces such as leather or cloth make poor fingerprint collectors.

3. Things. Objects made of hard and smooth materials like those of places hold a print well.

B. Extract. Investigators find and gather raw prints depending on how a person made them. Sometimes fingerprints provide a better option than DNA for identification in public scenes, and any others with a large population of persons even though DNA comes earlier in the processing order. Unless the investigator employs a single-use brush and powder for each scene, he will cross contaminate the scene with brushes and dust, by possibly picking up DNA laden material and spreading it to other areas.

Fingerprints have oils from a person's hands and present a possible source of DNA. The investigator decides which to pursue before exposing the scene to fingerprinting.

1. Basic. If the investigator has no ALS or laser, she can use powder to make the prints visible (patent). Fine powder on smooth surfaces sticks to the sweat and oils to make the pattern visible and collectible by clear tape. The investigator mounts the tape with the print onto a card with details about the case.

The investigator takes images of all prints to document them in an overview, intermediate, and close up; with and without a scale sticker, and orientation information. The camera's macro lens focuses close enough to the prints to show lines, features, and patterns. The investigator may not need powder to make the image visible, but powder prevents her from covering the latent print with a sticker by accident. This method of never touching the print can avoid the risks of mechanical error in lifting prints.

2. Cyanoacrylate provides another option to make fingerprint patterns in oil both permanent, and visible. The technique requires a sealed environment for the operator to place an item in called a fuming chamber. The chamber heats the superglue and raises the humidity in the closed space. The glue particles stick to the oils and moisture in the fingerprints and create permanent fingerprints. The investigator processes the prints with photography or basic powder and tape.

3. Heptane Ninhydrin develops fingerprints on paper, such as checks or other documents. The investigator sprays the items with a solution which reacts with the amino acids in the oils in the fingerprints to create a purple fingerprint. A warm humid environment helps the reaction. The procedure makes the prints visible for a short time, so the investigator photographs the prints with a scale for comparison, and preservation.

4. Polyvinylsiloxane works well to preserve fingerprints on rough surfaces like window sills bearing ridges from repeated coats of paints and brush marks. The investigator applies the material via a tool like a caulking gun to cover uneven surfaces and collect the print after dusting. Polyvinylsiloxane gel covers the dusted prints on rough or contoured surfaces where tape does contact all parts of the surface. The lab techs use the silicone for comparison.

C. Preserve. Investigators preserve fingerprints on cards, images, casting such as polyvinylsiloxane, or sometimes the item itself as in the case of a heptane ninhydrin developed print.

D. Process. After collection of the raw prints, investigators send their prints to a fingerprint lab often called Central Identification for comparison. Some departments with high demand have their own in house labs, while smaller departments contract with regional labs for their prints. Laboratories seek matches for blind fingerprints in public scenes, whereas they refuse blind DNA testing with its high expense for low payout. Fingerprint labs can process fingerprint returns faster, and with a much lower cost compared to DNA. Fingerprint technicians compare the collected prints with identified exemplars stored in IAFIS. Technicians with advanced training use equipment to analyze the components of prints, and compare prints to known samples to identify persons.

1. Refine. Modern fingerprint examination digitizes prints into images. This allows significant automation of the process of comparison to get potential matches for a person to compare.

2. Standardize. Fingerprints vary in quality by the number of features, and clarity of the print, both the original, and the collection. Scale helps to achieve this so the machines can match patterns along with sizing.

3. Interpret. The investigator sets the search parameters for local, or nationwide. Technicians classify prints in three categories: a match, rule someone in, or rule someone out. The two decisive designations make investigations easy, but the middle designation means the investigator has a potential candidate requiring corroboration.

E. Technical Admissibility. Fingerprints to meet the standards of Daubert and Frye in order for admission to court. Most state of the art processes have approval in a court somewhere. The admissibility falls back to the investigator's procedural adherence.

E. Legal Admissibility. Most fingerprints come from victim controlled scenes with outstanding suspects, making their legal admissibility simple.

II. Evidence Analysis

A. Cause. Fingerprint evidence comes from a person's accidental and functional behavior when suspects often have tasks in mind to accomplish in the course of the crime. Some persons make fingerprints out of habit, such as touching things.

B. Creation. When a person transfers the skin ridge patterns by the oils on his hands to a hard and often smooth surface he creates invisible prints. Persons make fingerprint evidence by touching surfaces with their hands. Persons produce fingerprint evidence when they leave the friction ridge patterns on their fingers and hands on other scenes by touching them. Most persons secrete sweat and oils from their hands as a medium to transfer the pattern. Fingerprints come from specific hand touch interactions, and unlike DNA, fingerprints have no spill factor to spread them, although persons or other forces move objects with fingerprints.

1. Construction Fingerprints come as construction evidence. The person's print adds to the existing scene to create the evidence.

2. Deconstruction Fingerprint evidence does not deconstruct from the person. The fingerprint remains on the person, although the oils transferring the pattern (and containing DNA) deconstruct from a person.

3. Transfer. Fingerprint evidence goes from the person's hand as the origin site to the surface he touches. Fingerprints remain in their introduction and synthesis spot after placement, but they can rest on portable surfaces. A person transfers his fingerprint patterns by the sweat which reproduced the patterns on friction ridges. Hard and smooth surfaces like glass or countertops make excellent materials to accept the pattern.

III. Evidence to Proof

A. Strengths. Fingerprints prove the identity of the person whose hand touched a scene. Fingerprints provide direct evidence of identification and sometimes indirect evidence as actions.

1. Accuracy. Fingerprint evidence identifies someone by a person's hands or fingers. This evidence provides biometric identification of a hand which contacted a surface and indicates actions. The person had a reason to touch the surface, which may not solve a crime, but can help the investigator know where to look for evidence. A fingerprint's role as identifying evidence also includes action evidence. An investigator identifies the body part associated with the sample. Handling means control and possession. Fingerprints tell more than biological material in some ways. Without serology, DNA comes from less specific contact and needs further work to clarify where the DNA came from. The fingerprints in any particular spot come from the person who last touched the spot. Fingerprints go beyond identification to indicate key areas, and sometimes how a person controlled a scene. Their closeness to the center of gravity, point of entry o point of exit relates to involvement by presence. The evidence provides the fact of a specific person's body touching and possible controlling another scene with hands which defines more about the case than DNA. Fingerprints do not move after emplacement.

2. Uniqueness. Everyone so far has unique fingerprints. Fingerprints have features, like DNA has its alphabet of letters. The more features in common between two fingerprints, in the same configuration, the stronger the match. The features must also have the same arrangement of features for matching. Those two factors make fingerprints unique.

Fingerprints have three main design components: loops (most common), whorls (somewhat common), and arches (rarest). Those features also have subcategories. DNA has its alphabet, fingerprint classification has one too. Examiners classify fingerprints by their features in order to help fingerprint examiners narrow the possible matches. Then they compare them to see if they match in their features, and configuration by relative locations of the features. A technician looks for at least 12 common features, but some agencies have higher standards, such as 16 matching features, or as high as 20.

3. Proof Ability. A print from a scene can only aid an investigation if matched to a person. Fingerprint databases have far more files than DNA databases. Every DNA profile has a fingerprint profile for arrestees, while not all fingerprint files have a related DNA file. A smaller scene or article with limited interaction points provides a good chance of determining who touched a surface last.

B. Weaknesses. Fingerprint evidence has limits from its fragility as well its specific requirements for creation. Persons' fingerprints provide identification only coming from a person's hands. Fingerprints have no proximity deposits like DNA. Fingerprints only help the investigator determine relative time frames. They obliterate prior prints in the same location. This limitation works to present recent interaction but also means the investigation loses out on identifying a relevant suspect who touched the surface earlier.

1. Vulnerability. Fingerprint evidence has some overlap with biological evidence for its vulnerability. The longer the prints remain exposed the more potential damage to them. Fingerprints built on oils in a person's hand can dry out over time.

a. Environment. Weather can damage fingerprints, and dry out the oils holding the print. Fire can also dry out and destroy fingerprints. Latent prints from the oils in sweat dry up, and the print disappears. Children have different chemical make ups in their sweat, making it more vulnerable to drying up.

b. Person. Persons can destroy prints with ease by wiping them away, or covering them with new prints.

2. Countermeasures. A person wearing gloves prevents depositing his fingerprints on a scene, while DNA sloughs off a person all the time and in many different forms.

3. Proof Inability. Fingerprints can identify a person, and maybe provide a limited timeline. Considered alone, they cannot prove what a person did unless on a control point.

A specific person's lack of fingerprints at a scene has multiple possible explanations including lack of presence, lack of contact, or the person wore gloves to block fingerprints. Some persons do not secrete oils from their hands to leave fingerprints. Their fingerprints are limited to using mediums like blood or soft receiving materials. The lack of a specific person's fingerprints at a scene without additional information only means she did not find the person's fingerprints at the scene. She needs more information from additional evidence to conclude presence or lack of presence.

The enormous nationwide IAFIS database has the limit of only including persons arrested by police, perhaps a fifth or sixth of the population, which leaves out international suspects, and persons with not prior arrests. The system excludes military fingerprints, teachers, and perhaps juveniles. Some suspects have no criminal history and no prints on file, requiring the investigator obtain the suspect's prints for comparison. Fingerprints have no equivalent to familial DNA.

C. Reinforcing Evidence. The investigator can reinforce latent fingerprints by providing strong documentation and other connected evidence.

1. Documentary. The investigator strengthens the evidence with information including date, time, location, orientation or the prints, who took the print, and by what method.

2. Corroboration. Evidence redundancy for identification increases the odds of solving the case. Information and images provide context to fingerprints' identification abilities. This becomes more useful with complex evidence situations allowing an investigator to cover all areas of basic facts including identification, presence, action, control, and impact.

3.5.2 WORKING PATENT FINGERPRINTS

Investigators use patent fingerprints to identify specific persons from visible patterns to support the investigation.

Goal. The investigator seeks to find and collect patent fingerprints for an expert to identify the person who produced them, and develop information about the touching means.

I. Evidence Collection

A. Find. The investigator finds visible patent fingerprints easier to find than invisible latent prints. Patent fingerprints production process makes immediately visible eliminating and reducing the search efforts. They show up in the same places as latent prints, with the exception of far more robustness on persons.

1. Persons. Persons and their clothing items can receive and hold patent prints in blood as an ink with more success than the person could with oils. A living or dead person can capture the bloody print on his skin or even on cloth. Investigators can collect prints off living persons without coordination with the Medical Examiner.

2. Places. Patent fingerprints in places center on interaction points for a person's hands, like door handles, light switches, and faucets where a person tries to clean up.

3. Things. Patent fingerprints on articles like objects and tools show the relevance to the case. If the material holding the print like blood has a direct connection to the crime, it connects the object to a person along with actions.

B. Extract. Investigators collect paten prints by photographing the evidence, and collecting it. Investigators collect patent prints by photographic methods, using

ALS to enhance visibility. Some prints contrast enough with the background to not need fingerprint powder for visibility. These uneven surfaces present challenges with using traditional powder and tape. Polyvinylsiloxane also works well to collect patent fingerprints given they come in three dimensions on uneven surfaces. Polyvinylsiloxane produces an impression mold of fingerprints.

C. Preserve. Investigators preserve patent fingerprints by images and collecting the items holding the print.

D. Process. Technicians process patent prints the same as latent prints with the use of a lab and data systems.

1. Refine. Investigator in the field or the technician digitizes prints into images with scale to automate the process.

2. Standardize. The technician size adjusts the scaled fingerprints.

3. Interpret. The technician seeks a match for the prints.

E. Technical Admissibility. Patent fingerprints meet the standards of Daubert and Frye in order for admission to court.

E. Legal Admissibility. Most patent fingerprints come from the same victim related places as latent prints, simplifying their legal admissibility.

II. Evidence Analysis

A. Cause. Patent fingerprint evidence often stems from accidental creation with a medium such as blood. Persons touch things out of intentional purpose, sometimes by accident, and habit.

B. Creation. Persons create patent fingerprints in the same ways as latent prints with construction, and transference. , but this method relies on transferring the medium from a source to the person's hands, to the receiving scene where the person deposits the prints.

III. Evidence to Proof

A. Strengths. Fingerprints prove the identity of the person whose hand touched a scene. Fingerprints are physical evidence which provide direct evidence of identification, and indications to activity as indirect evidence. Fingerprint technicians compare the collected prints with identified exemplars stored in IAFIS. Fingerprint evidence has limits from its fragility as well as its specificity. Persons' fingerprints provide identification only coming from a person's hands. A person wearing gloves prevents depositing his fingerprints on a scene, while DNA sloughs off a person all the time and in many different forms. Fingerprints have no proximity deposits like DNA. Fingerprints only help the investigator determine relative time frames by obliterating prior prints in the same location. This limitation works to present recent interaction but also means the investigation loses out on identifying a relevant suspect who touched the surface earlier.

Fingerprint analysis helps identify a potential suspect regardless of scene. The investigator considers the timing of print production as before, during, or after the crime. Fingerprints have limited and varying resilience. Latent prints imprinted in the oils in sweat dry up, and the print disappears. Children have different chemical make ups in their sweat, making it more vulnerable to drying up. Patent prints in a medium such as blood have far more resistance. Stable materials like clay offer plastic prints of high resilience.

1. Accuracy. Patent fingerprints have the same accuracy as latent prints.

2. Uniqueness. Patent fingerprints have the same uniqueness as latent fingerprints.

3. Proof Ability. Patent fingerprints can prove the same things as latent prints, but they can also provide a relative timeline. A fingerprint in the blood at a stabbing scene implies the person touched the spilled blood then created the print where the investigator found it. A bloody fingerprint alone does not prove guilt as bystanders may rush to help a person and make patent prints also.

B. Weaknesses. Patent prints can prove identification, and add in a connected medium, but they cannot make the whole case.

1. Vulnerability. Fingerprint evidence has some overlap with biological evidence for its vulnerability.

a. Environment. Weather can damage patent fingerprints, and wash away the medium. Wind, sun, and fire can dry the medium and destroy it. Patent prints in a medium such as blood have far more resistance to the environment, but can wash away.

b. Person. Persons can destroy patent fingerprints by cleaning the scene.

2. Countermeasures. Persons avoid patent fingerprints by gloves like they do latent prints. They can also avoid paten prints by avoiding a medium to transfer the prints.

3. Proof Inability. Patent fingerprints cannot prove everything. A bloody print can come from a bystander providing first aid.

C. Reinforcing Evidence. Patent fingerprints need documentary and corroborating evidence to strengthen them for court.

1. Documentary. The investigator obtains all the information she would with a latent print including methods of discovery and collection, but also adding identification of the medium of the prints.

2. Corroboration. Patent fingerprints require all the corroborating evidence as latent fingerprints. If the investigator knows the medium comes from the suspect, collecting some for DNA could corroborate identifying evidence.

3.5.3 WORKING PLASTIC FINGERPRINTS

Investigators use plastic fingerprints to identify specific persons from three dimensional patterns to support the investigation.

Goal. The investigator seeks to find and collect plastic fingerprints to match with established records, identify the producing person, and determine specific actions of touching the scene.

I. Evidence Collection

A. Find. While the investigator finds latent and patent fingerprints at interaction points with hard, smooth, and sometimes absorbent material, she finds plastic fingerprints at interaction points where of soft material like clay. While rare, these prints solve cases.

1. Persons. Human body does not have soft material to take a plastic print.

2. Places. Construction sites have soft material able to collect prints. Kitchens also contain some foods which have the same soft properties.

3. Things. Cement, putty, and cake frosting act as good mediums to collect plastic prints.

B. Extract. Investigators may find plastic prints fragile depending on the material. The investigator photographs the print first. Lighting the print from the side can make the ridge pattern clear. The investigator uses polyvinylsiloxane casting to extracting a plastic print on uneven surfaces. The investigator can also collect the 3D print from the scene if possible.

C. Preserve. Investigators preserve plastic fingerprints by photographs, castings, and the print itself.

D. Process. Technicians digitize the prints in the lab and process them the same way as with the other print types.

E. Technical Admissibility. Collect plastic fingerprints to meet the standards of Daubert and Frye in order for admission to court when the investigator shows the process reproduced the print with accuracy.

E. Legal Admissibility. Most plastic fingerprints have the same legal admissibility requirements as other prints.

II. Evidence Analysis

A. Cause. Plastic fingerprints come from a person's contact with soft materials. Most persons make accidental contact, but a person could leave fingerprints on cake frosting while eating.

B. Creation. Persons make three dimensional plastic fingerprints by touching soft material and leaving a mold of the ridge pattern in the material. Persons construct plastic fingerprints when he transfers the pattern and the hand modifies the receiving material into a three dimensional representation of the fingerprint.

III. Evidence to Proof

A. Strengths. Plastic fingerprints offer all the strengths for a case as other prints, but with a potential for more precise time estimation.

1. Accuracy. Plastic fingerprints have all the accuracy as latent and patent fingerprints.

2. Uniqueness. Plastic fingerprints have all the uniqueness as latent and patent fingerprints, but may also connect the print donor with particular behavior, such as eating frosted cake inside a burglary scene.

3. Proof Ability. Plastic fingerprints can provide a relative timeline. Most matter does not exist in a permanent state of soft and plastic prints may provide an indication of when something happened in addition to contact.

B. Weaknesses. Plastic fingerprints present challenges to the investigator trying to collect and use the print.

1. Vulnerability. The soft material holding the print may accept other prints afterward, destroying the important ones.

a. Environment. Weather can damage plastic fingerprints like the others.

b. Person. Persons often destroy plastic fingerprints by not realizing the material remains soft.

2. Countermeasures. Suspects use the same countermeasures for plastic fingerprints as with other fingerprints. Gloves prevent the patterns from transfer. They can also damage the scenes after to destroy prints, or take items bearing their prints with them.

3. Proof Inability. Like the other fingerprints, plastic prints can only identify a person, and maybe provide a limited timeline.

C. Reinforcing Evidence. Plastic fingerprints require the same reinforcement as all other fingerprints.

1. Documentary. The investigator documents all the details about the plastic fingerprint, including the material holding the print, and how she collected it.

2. Corroboration. Plastic fingerprints need corroboration like the other fingerprints.

3.6 WORKING PATTERNS

Patterns offer evidence to identify interacting scenes. Patterns come in three types:

3.6.1 Visual Physical Patterns

3.6.2 Chemical Patterns

3.6.3 Information Patterns

Goal. The investigator seeks pattern evidence to show scene interactions and identification in an investigation.

3.6.1 WORKING VISUAL PHYSICAL PATTERNS

Investigators use visual physical patterns to identify specific scenes from visual and three dimensional patterns to support the investigation.

Goal. The investigator seeks to find and collect visual physical patterns to match with established records, identify the connected scenes, and determine specific actions of the scenes when they created the pattern.

I. Evidence Collection

A. Find. Any scene makes a pattern visual or physical mark on another scene during an interaction. The investigator must see the pattern prior to collection. Conventional lighting, oblique lighting, and ALS aid in making pattern marks visible. A magnifying glass helps. Pattern quality relies on how much of a pattern exists to compare. More matching features offer better matches.

1. Persons. Scenes can imprint patterns on persons in the form of bruises, fractures, and bite marks. Dead persons may take on patterns of what they rest on, developing a visual pattern on the skin of livor mortis, where the blood pooled.

2. Places. Scenes imprint patterns on places most often in the form of physical patterns like pry marks, shoe prints or tread marks.

3. Things. Scenes imprint pattern marks on things with physical and visual marks in the same manner as with places. Some questioned documents have visual physical patterns on them an expert can analyze.

B. Extract. Investigators have the challenge of collecting patterns from scenes to make them available for examination and comparison. The production style and materials dictates how an investigator collects pattern marks. Investigators photograph marks like all other evidence, and collect the patterns either by scaled photography, impression mold, of tape lift like fingerprints.

1. Visual Patterns. Two dimensional visual patterns can work like writing, with one scene impressing its mark onto another. Latent and patent fingerprints act like visual patterns. Investigators use photographs or video to collect visual patterns. Investigators collect the item or surface holding the pattern or photograph the scene with a scale and orientation information to compare them under a microscope, and by sensitive instruments if necessary. Investigators match crime scene fingerprints to exemplar prints by their similar common features.

2. Physical Patterns. Three dimensional physical patterns work like a stamp on a forged tool, with one scene impressing its mark into another. Physical patterns connect scenes by three dimensional patterns created when one scene leaves its impression on another scene. Investigators collect physical patterns such as sections of damaged wood. The investigator photographs, then takes a mold of the impression with the same polyvinylsiloxane, plaster, or any substance molding to the shape of another surface. Photographs preserve physical patterns well. They capture features and details to show how they looked at a point in time.

C. Preserve. A camera preserves visual and physical patterns in two dimensions. Polyvinylsiloxane, plaster of Paris, and dental stone produce an impression mold for three dimensions. Collecting the pattern provides the best form as the investigator always has the original.

D. Process. Patterns may require low or high technology matching processes depending on the sophistication of the pattern. The investigator or technician must have both the scenes in order to match patterns, the scene making the mark, and the scene receiving it.

1. Refine. The investigator locates and isolates the pattern and what it includes.

2. Standardize. If the investigator collected the patterns by photography, then the technician must equalize the scale.

3. Interpret. After collection of visual physical patterns the investigator often looks at the patterns by microscope to compare features in two or three dimensions. Pattern matching as an umbrella concept relies on finding the class characteristics of patterns and the individual characteristics in order to match marks to what made them. Technicians compare visual patterns by identifying shared features. Blood spatter examiners evaluate visual patterns in blood to provide opinions about what happened, such as speed of weaponry, type of maneuver, and number of maneuvers. Technicians compare two scenes by microscope or enlarged photograph to look at the same features.

E. Technical Admissibility. The courts use the Daubert and Frye standards to measure the investigator's pattern evidence for admission to court. Good collection practices lead to admissibility.

F. Legal Admissibility. The investigator still needs the legal right to collect the evidence.

II. Evidence Analysis

A. Cause. Pattern marks come as the result of one scene imprinting a mark on another. The more resilient scene has the role of origin scene, while the softer scene has the role of synthesis and discovery scenes. Patterns vary in resilience from millennia old hieroglyphics or cave paintings to web applications which destroy all records of a communication in seconds. Pattern evidence brings two parts together at synthesis site and the two create a pattern. Most visual physical patterns come about from an intentional act such as prying a door, or walking across a floor. Persons who make pattern marks may also create them as byproducts for functional acts.

1. Construction. Scenes create construction evidence when a scene modifies another scene. Visual patterns connect scenes by the same visual patterns in two dimensions. They can work like a mirror image with a stamp, or have stylistic resemblance as in handwriting. Several facts contribute to the marking including velocities, mass, hardness, and inertia.

B. Creation. . The investigator inspects the pattern making scene to find evidence connecting it to a specific person who controlled it. Some scenes have pattern marks on them as the result of interacting with scenes capable of leaving a copy of a design. A scene makes a pattern when two scenes come together and one leaves a pattern on the other. Pattern makers include teeth, outlines of shapes, images. Patterns have uniqueness for an investigator to distinguish and identify them. Scenes produce or accept patterns depending on their material and hardness relative to the other scene

III. Evidence to Proof

A. Strengths. Pattern mark evidence provides detailed or limited facts of identification, presence, action, control, and damage.

1. Accuracy. Pattern mark evidence has excellent accuracy in identifying two parts of an interaction. Most scenes have unique features to identify them, but the investigator must determine the scale to do so. The challenge for the investigator centers on enhancing the patterns by scale. Pattern evidence can provide matches between scene interactions when no person has involvement. Patterns can show physical and documentary evidence in both direct and indirect forms.

2. Uniqueness. The more unique the pattern, the more proof ability it has. Pattern evidence includes any item able to make a mark, and an investigator with the right tools magnifies the mark to the point of uniqueness.

3. Proof Ability. Patterns can connect two interacting scenes by the mark one made on the other. Forensic dentists have used bite marks used to identify persons. Some court cases have resulted in discrediting the bite marks discipline. Patterns

provide identification facts to an investigator when used to connect two scenes. The evidence provides the fact of a specific scene's imprint on another scene. These patterns have the specificity of DNA or fingerprints, but lack the ability to identify the person controlling the scene which made the pattern. Connecting the pattern making scenes advances an investigation, but still requires connecting the pattern making to the controller.

B. Weaknesses. Peripheral pattern evidence has limited abilities to identify suspect and victim actions for investigations. It can provide a link between a person and other scenes, but often an investigator can find a shorter path between a person and another scene.

1. Vulnerability. Pattern mark evidence has vulnerabilities related to how it metamorphosed. The materials holding the patterns indicate the pattern's vulnerability over time. Left alone, visual and physical patterns last a long time but forces can act upon them.

a. Environment. Visual and physical patterns have high vulnerability depending on the material of the pattern. Patterns on stone have less vulnerability than patterns in snow.

b. Person. A person can destroy physical and visual patterns by force and chemical patterns by corrupting the material samples.

2. Countermeasures. Many visual physical patterns involve force, such as prying a door, and the marks become unavoidable. Persons may take or destroy pattern receiving scenes and evidence to prevent their use as evidence.

3. Proof Inability. Pattern marks lack precision of other matching evidence like DNA and fingerprints for lack of standardization. Pattern mark evidence cannot identify a person except perhaps with dental patterns, and handwriting (graphology).

Many times the suspect controlled scene of the two involved in the pattern making remains out of the investigator's grasp. The lack of standardized databases for the huge variety of patterns means the investigator needs both scenes to match them. Some places have robust databases of shoeprints, but unless investigators support the program by collecting patterns at crime scenes and during booking, the odds making of an unknown match remain low. The investigator overcomes the lack of a searchable database by developing other evidence to get to the pattern mark evidence.

C. Reinforcing Evidence. Visual physical patterns provide evidence often a link or two away from the persons in a case. Reinforcing evidence allows the investigator to create the chain connecting persons to the pattern making scenes.

1. Documentary. Pattern marks require documentation evidence for context. Many times documentary evidence allows the investigator to make the connections between the pattern evidence and other evidence.

2. Corroboration. Pattern mark evidence has a limited group of companion evidence as it has the least use among the six evidence types. The use of other the other identifying evidence types of DNA and fingerprints connecting to scenes with pattern marks can corroborate the pattern marks' evidence.

3.6.2 WORKING CHEMICAL PATTERNS

Investigators use chemical patterns to identify specific scenes by their chemical formula to support the investigation.

Goal. The investigator seeks to find and collect chemical patterns to match with established records, identify the connected scenes, and determine specific actions of the scenes making the pattern.

I. Evidence Collection

A. Find. Chemicals can show up at any scene in the form of liquids, solids, or gases on any scene including persons, places, or thins. The investigator only needs to recognize their significance. The chemical pattern connects the matter to other scenes.

B. Extract. Investigators collect chemical patterns by gathering material in packaging designed to protect it.

C. Preserve. Chemical collection tools like glass jars, or other appropriate packaging aid in chemical patterns.

D. Process. Chemical patterns require high technology matching.

1. Refine. The investigator or technician refines the substance by isolating it for testing.

2. Standardize. The technician examining material for chemical patterns uses validated testing methods to establish the identification of the chemical.

3. Interpret. The technician may identify the chemical or establish a chemical match to another sample. Matter has a chemical recipe of its composition. When an investigator finds an unidentified chemical she can decipher the pattern. The

chemical's identity can help indicate its context for the case. Chemical patterns connect scenes by the formula of a material. Technicians work with chemical patterns and identify the exact material with contextual clues and defined chemicals like drugs, or explosives. A drug metabolizes into known chemicals. Technicians look at the product of metabolized drugs and reverse engineer the reaction to identify the original chemical. Every piece of matter has a chemical formula to identify and define it.

E. Technical Admissibility. The courts use the Daubert and Frye standards to measure the investigator's chemical pattern evidence for admission to court.

F. Legal Admissibility. The investigator needs the legal right to collect the evidence.

II. Evidence Analysis

A. Cause. Events in cases cause chemical pattern involvement when the investigator needs to know the composition of a substance. Most chemicals in scenes have intentional involvement as they serve a function, such as drugs, or gasoline.

B. Creation. The mechanics of most chemical pattern creation take place before the crime, but sometimes persons in crime create chemicals as part of the events.

1. Construction. Scenes construct chemical pattern evidence when chemicals come from different places to combine as part of the crime, such as making drugs. Drugs have specific chemicals which define them, sometimes making the difference between legal and illegal substances.

2. Deconstruction. Chemical patterns deconstruct such as when a body metabolizes drugs. Investigators and technicians seek the waste from the body's processing the drugs to identify the presence of the drug in a person.

3. Transfer. Most cases involve the transference of chemical patterns from one scene to another, such as pouring gasoline on an arson target.

III. Evidence to Proof

A. Strengths. Chemical pattern mark evidence can define an exact chemical for an investigation. The definition can identify or match multiple samples of a chemical to link scenes.

1. Accuracy. Technicians use laboratory analysis tests to perform chemical pattern comparisons such as bringing certain chemicals in contact with the suspect chemicals and recording reactions. Lab technicians practice this recognition with greater complexity by reverse engineering formulas to discover what chemicals interacted to result in the evidence.

2. Uniqueness. Investigators identify and differentiate paint chips, glass, or other materials by their chemical patterns which dictate some of their features.

3. Proof Ability. Defining chemicals gives the investigator the ability to prove interaction between scenes.

B. Weaknesses. Chemical patterns like visual physical pattern have some distance from the person scenes an investigator needs to chain together to prove a case.

1. Vulnerability. The stability of chemical pattern mark evidence represents its vulnerabilities. Chemicals degrade, and information patterns need away to store them making their survival over time varying. As with trace evidence, the chemicals may migrate also.

a. Environment. Chemical patterns interact with other chemicals to change. Oxidation changes physical patterns.

b. Person. A person can destroy chemical patterns by corrupting the material samples or cleaning them.

2. Countermeasures. Suspects may clean scenes and eliminate or obscure chemical patterns.

3. Proof Inability. Chemical patterns cannot prove identification of persons like DNA or fingerprints can. The modern world puts persons in contact with many chemicals in daily life, from cleaners to medications.

C. Reinforcing Evidence. Chemical patterns matching requires a variety of measures to reinforce its value as evidence including explaining it, and backing it up.

1. Documentary. Chemical pattern evidence needs all the documentation of visual physical patterns, with additional details about the chemical science.

2. Corroboration. Chemical pattern evidence obtains strong corroboration from identification evidence such as DNA or fingerprints. Those evidence types connect the actions associated with the chemicals to a person.

3.6.3 WORKING INFORMATION PATTERNS

Investigators use information patterns to identify specific scenes by their arrangement of information to support the investigation.

Goal. The investigator uses information patterns to seek and collect information to match with established records, identify the connected scenes, and determine specific actions of scenes.

I. Evidence Collection

A. Find. Persons configure letters and numbers from the alphabet into meaningful collections. The word or pattern of letters, *car* means a machine a person drives, with wheels, a power source. These information patterns represent reality, and the investigator can use information patterns to identify parts of scenes, evidence, and dynamics. Informational patterns connect scenes by a string of data.

1. Persons. Persons have thousands of attributes and gathering them together forms a pattern, such as a description of fugitive. If the investigator uses enough features like hair color, eye color, height, weight, skin tone, gender, the pattern can make a unique profile of the person. Sequenced DNA comes with an informational pattern.

2. Places. Hosting scenes can also have thousands of features like a person to make them unique.

3. Things. The proliferation of information tools has created opportunities to work with information patterns beyond the traditional words and numbers on a page. Double entry accounting creates a pattern where the account enters the figure leaving one account, and entering another. Phone numbers, email addresses, and passwords all relate to information patterns. Informational patterns also identify machines when they exchange information. Informational patterns provide print-

outs of what happened with the information exchange. Persons use a password to restrict access to their smartphone and its computer applications, thus reducing the suspect pool.

B. Extract. Information pattern evidence comes in patterns to make it universal. Some information has specificity to the point where the investigation could use the patterns to identify connections between scenes. Investigators collect vast amounts of information during an investigation. The investigator recognizes information has significance to investigations and collects it by recording it in writing, images, or computer files.

C. Preserve. Informational patterns require information tools to collect patterns. They range from pencil and paper to supercomputers.

D. Process. Patterns may require low or high technology matching.

1. Refine. The investigator finds information patterns and defines them, such as a series of features, or a string of information. Technicians use computers for complex informational comparisons with large amounts of data. An investigator exports an entire database to a spreadsheet to search the cells for particular strings, such as numbers, or particular words.

2. Standardize. Most information patterns come in written form, and the investigator defines the pattern. Patterns could come in sound form like a song or visual form like an image on street sign indicating wildlife, or even light such as using a signal light for Morse Code.

3. Interpret. An investigator or technician can identify or interpret two pieces of information as a match by comparing the two on paper, or using an information machine to do so.

E. Technical Admissibility. The courts assess how the investigator obtained and compared information using the Daubert and Frye standards to ensure the processes adhere to science.

F. Legal Admissibility. Pattern evidence comes from somewhere and the investigator must show legal right to collect the evidence.

II. Evidence Analysis

A. Cause. Information pattern evidence comes as a representation of reality expressed in words or numbers. The parts of information within the pattern can have roots in randomness or accident, but the movement of the pattern comes by design.

B. Creation. Information patterns come about by construction and transference. A scene can create information on its own, or by combining multiple sources. Information patterns move from one scene to another. Evidence in information form combines data to produce a larger string of data which an investigator compares with others to determine patterns. Investigators work with person names as informational patterns. Sequenced DNA becomes an informational pattern. Persons use passwords as patterns to access a computer program like email, or a bank account. Informational patterns also identify machines when they exchange information. Informational patterns provide printouts of what happened with the information exchange. Persons use a password to restrict access to their smartphone and its computer applications, thus reducing the suspect pool.

III. Evidence to Proof

A. Strengths. Information patterns acting as representations of reality can distill facts to simple form to make connections between scenes. Information patterns can save time, such as in the case where CODIS has DNA sequenced.

1. Accuracy. Information pattern evidence can come with high accuracy with longer strings of information.

2. Uniqueness. Information patterns with greater detail have higher uniqueness.

3. Proof Ability. As distillations of other evidence, information patterns can prove anything.

B. Weaknesses. Information pattern evidence has weaknesses of other patterns as it represents other evidence.

1. Vulnerability. Information pattern evidence's vulnerabilities stem from its role as a representation of reality. Information patterns need a way to store them making their survival over time varying.

a. Environment. Information patterns' vulnerability to the environment centers on what holds the information and conditions. Electronic information has susceptibility to power issues. Whatever happens to the original scene or evidence can impact the patterns of information.

b. Person. Persons can destroy information patterns stored on traditional sources like all other evidence. Persons can also clear an information tool of its patterns with little or no effort.

2. Countermeasures. A suspect's countermeasures with information patterns centers on disrupting the matching process by destroying evidence, or changing details.

3. Proof Inability. Information patterns often have a separation between it and person evidence meaning it may not prove an identity.

C. Reinforcing Evidence. The investigator can reinforce information pattern evidence in the same ways as with other patterns.

1. Documentary. Information patterns may have easy to document information about the evidence and how the investigator found and processed it.

2. Corroboration. As the information pattern evidence represents other evidence, the investigator should cover all the evidence distilled into the information patterns.

CHAPTER 4. INVESTIGATION EVALUATION

The end of an investigative cycle prompts the investigator to evaluate the investigation report presenting the investigation to the world. The decisive investigator decides how to evaluate the investigation by applying functional goals as methods to proving who did what. The investigator looks at the four methods of objectivity, proof, direction and writing with the different component investigations in every case. Evaluating takes far less time and effort than production.

The evaluation of the thematic sub investigations come in a different order than presented in the organizing section of the first chapter. The evaluation becomes stronger in a different order when the investigator avoids following the same path taken to get there. The change in order demands the evaluator determine if the case can still prove who did what.

How to evaluate an investigation?

The investigator evaluates the whole case, and the seven sub-investigations for its ability to prove who did what. The report provides a distilled product of the investigation for the investigator to evaluate his decisions and the outcomes to understand the case better. The evaluation comes in the framework of the four functional goals of objectivity, facts, direction, and writing.

Goal. Did the investigator define the component and address it with objectivity, facts, direction, and writing?

I. Objectivity

A. Open Mindedness. Does the report indicate the investigator's openness to all facts, evidence and ideas while also accepting the case ambiguities?

B. Reasoning. Does the report show the investigator approached matters with logical thinking to prove points and establish facts?

C. Bias Awareness. Does the report show the investigator recognized bias as a threat to a quality investigation, took steps to overcome it, and focused on fact-based reasoning?

II. Facts

A. Individual. Does the report include facts from evidence proving the five capabilities in the following ways?

1. Identity.

2. Presence.

3. Interaction.

4. Control.

5. Impact.

B. Group. Does the report validate facts by grouping similar evidence relating to base subject of the investigator's actions for its independence, corroboration, or refutation and present evidence in the following ways?

1. Independent evidence without corroboration.

2. Corroborating evidence to cross validate facts.

3. Refuting evidence showing countering facts.

C. Collective. Does the report show the investigator considered the total body of evidence in a case to determine culpability in the following ways?

1. Rule out.

2. Rule in.

3. Deem exculpable.

4. Deem culpable.

III. Direction

A. Priorities. Does the report show the investigator conducted the case adhering to the principles of objectivity, proof, writing, and direction as well as the sub-investigations into evidence, scenes, laws, dynamics, victims, witnesses, and suspects for full coverage of the case?

1. Does the report show evidence to prove who did what?

2. Does the report show use of the four methods to organize the sub investigation?

3. Does the report show how the evidence sub investigation works with the six other themed sub investigations?

B. Status. Does the report evaluate whether the investigation met the parameters of proving who did what, and identifying evidence gaps to address with scenes?

1. Does the report meet the challenge to prove who did what?

2. Does the report fall short of meeting the challenge while producing usable evidence?

3. Does the report fail to provide any evidence to prove who did what?

C. Plans. Does the report identify the investigator's plan for what to do next by using the gaps in the status to try and meet the priorities of the case to decide what how to proceed?

1. Will the report go to the prosecutor to try the suspect?

2. Will the report go to another person or group for follow up investigation?

3. Will the investigator continue to work on the investigation in a different area?

4. Will the report go to the unsolved or close case file?

IV. Writing

A. Format. Does the report cover the investigator's actions by organizing the report in a logical order, making facts easy to find?

B. Descriptions. Does the report describe scenes, evidence, and activities in detail, with precision, accuracy, and plain language for clarity?

C. Grammar. Does the report show the investigator followed the proper usage standards of grammar with parts of speech including proper nouns, descriptive adjectives, active verbs, and few adverbs to cover the case by avoiding confusion?

D. Style. Does the report show the investigator wrote it with a clear first person style covering the facts in a flowing manner navigating through the topics?

4.1 EVALUATING SCENE INVESTIGATIONS

The report explains how scenes in a case have roles in evidence production. The outcomes of scene relationships provide the material for the investigator to reverse engineer the events. Scene investigations come first in evaluation. The investigator obtained the evidence from them, making them the root of the case.

Goal. Did the investigator define the scenes, and how the interacted to produce evidence?

I. Objectivity

A. Open Mindedness. Does the report cover all the available scenes in the investigator's decision of scene to focus on?

B. Reasoning. Does the report reflect the investigator's scene choice as a considered decision with the analysis and evidence work as continuations of logical choices?

C. Bias Awareness. Does the report reflect the absence of bias in scene choice and investigation?

II. Facts

A. Individual. Does the report show the involved scenes proving them with the facts in the following ways?

1. Identification.

2. Presence.

3. Interaction.

4. Possession or control.

5. Impact, damage or injury.

B. Group. Does the report validate facts by grouping similar evidence relating to base subject of the law for its independence, corroboration, or refutation and present evidence in the following ways?

1. Independent evidence to prove a fact about a scene without corroboration.

2. Corroborating evidence to validate facts about scenes.

3. Refuting evidence to show countering facts about scenes.

C. Collective. Does the report show the investigator considered the total body of evidence in a case to determine culpability by connecting scenes in the following ways?

1. Rule out.

2. Rule in.

3. Deem exculpable.

4. Deem culpable.

III. Direction

A. Priorities. Does the report how the scene choice related to connections and possible interactions?

B. Status. Does the report show how much evidence the scenes provide toward proving the case, and covering the investigative needs?

C. Plans. Does the report state the investigator's next step with scenes given the current status, including the next scene to investigate?

IV. Writing

A. Format. Does the report cover the scenes by organizing the report in a logical order, making facts easy to find?

B. Descriptions. Does the report describe scenes in detail with plain language making them clear?

C. Grammar. Does the report use language in a way to facilitate precise details about scenes including proper nouns, and active verbs to discuss the scenes?

D. Style. Does the report cover the scenes in an easy to read manner?

4.2 EVALUATING EVIDENCE INVESTIGATIONS

The report shows how evidence comes from scenes and converts into proof, and facts. The investigator evaluates the evidence after scene. Evidence comes from scenes and determines whether the investigator can prove who did what.

Goal. Did the investigator obtain evidence from the scenes to prove who did what?

I. Objectivity

A. Open Mindedness. Does the report show openness to all evidence?

B. Reasoning. Does the report reflect the logical and scientific thinking to prove facts?

C. Bias Awareness. Does the report show efforts to avoid bias as a threat to understanding evidence capabilities?

II. Facts

A. Individual. Does the report show how evidence proves the case with the facts in the following ways?

1. Identification of the scenes and evidence.

2. Presence.

3. Interactions.

4. Possession or control.

5. Impact as damage or injury.

B. Group. Does the report validate facts by grouping similar evidence relating to base subject of evidence for its independence, corroboration, or refutation and present evidence in the following ways?

1. Independent evidence to prove facts without corroboration.

2. Corroborating evidence to validate facts by using different evidence to prove the same facts in a base concept.

3. Refuting evidence to show countering facts.

C. Collective. Does the report show the investigator considered the total body of evidence in a case to determine culpability in the following ways?

1. Rule out.

2. Rule in.

3. Deem exculpable.

4. Deem culpable.

III. Direction

A. Priorities. Obtaining evidence is the case priority.

1. Does the evidence prove who did what?

2. Do the four methods help analyze the evidence?

3. Does the evidence interact with the other six themed sub investigations?

B. Status. The status of evidence controls the case.

1. Does the evidence meet the priorities?

2. Does the evidence fall short of meeting the case priorities?

3. Does the evidence fail to meet the case priorities?

C. Plans. The evidence plans revolve around the status compared to the priorities.

1. Does the report indicate plans for the evidence?

2. Does the report indicate plans to obtain more evidence?

IV. Writing

A. Format. Does the report organize the evidence in a logical order, covering evidence details, type, location, process?

B. Descriptions. Does the report describe evidence and the processes to obtain it in plain language with detail?

C. Grammar. Does the report use language like proper nouns and active verbs to make the writing about the evidence concise and detailed?

D. Style. Does the report use a clear first person narrative style to cover the evidence in a flowing manner?

4.3 EVALUATING CRIME DYNAMIC INVESTIGATIONS

The report demonstrates the investigator's knowledge of what happened in the case, from preparations, to actions, to recovery. Dynamics investigations connect evidence to show the actions among the involved persons and scenes.

Goal. Did the investigator define the dynamics of the case as cause and effect activity?

I. Objectivity

A. Open Mindedness. Does the report show openness to any crime dynamics?

B. Reasoning. Does the report reflect logical thinking to prove dynamics through facts?

C. Bias Awareness. Does the report show fairness overcoming potential biases by considering the dynamics with proven facts and avoiding preconceived ideas?

II. Facts

A. Individual. Does the report show the dynamics applicable to the case, and how to prove them with the facts in the following ways?

1. Identify every entity and action involved.

2. Presence.

3. Interaction.

4. Possession or control.

5. Damage or injury.

B. Group. Does the report validate facts about crime dynamics for its independence, corroboration, or refutation and present evidence in the following ways?

1. Independent evidence to prove a dynamic without corroboration.

2. Corroborating evidence validates facts relating to dynamics by using different evidence to prove the same facts in a base concept.

3. Refuting evidence to show countering facts about crime dynamics.

C. Collective. Does the report show the investigator considered the total body of evidence in a case to determine culpability for the crime dynamics in the following ways?

1. Rule out.

2. Rule in.

3. Deem exculpable.

4. Deem culpable.

III. Direction

A. Priorities. Does the report show the priorities of proving dynamics with evidence?

B. Status. Does the report show the case includes enough evidence to prove a person the dynamics in the case?

C. Plans. Does the report outline plans of what to do next considering the status compared to the priorities of the case?

IV. Writing

A. Format. Does the report's format cover the dynamics in an organized way to make the actions clear?

B. Descriptions. Does the report describe the crime dynamics with the facts?

C. Grammar. Does the report use proper nouns and active verbs to cover the dynamics in attributive form?

D. Style. Does the report style explain the crime dynamics in simple terms while removing jargon?

4.4 EVALUATING VICTIM INVESTIGATIONS

The report always defines the victim and the outcome on the victim. The investigator evaluates the victim as the first person of the three person types. The courts shift emphasis from what happened to the victim to proving the suspect's actions.

Goal. Did the investigator define the victim, the victim's actions, and how the suspect impacted the victim by the crime?

I. Objectivity

A. Open Mindedness. Does the report consider alternate ideas and courses for the victim with ambiguous evidence?

B. Reasoning. Does the report show investigator approached the victim with logical evidence based thinking to prove points?

C. Bias Awareness. Does the report take a neutral approach avoiding bias toward the victims?

II. Facts

A. Individual. Does the report show how to prove the victim's activities with the facts in the following ways?

1. Identification.

2. Presence.

3. Interactions.

4. Possession or control of other entities.

5. Impact, damage or injury.

B. Group. Does the report validate facts by grouping similar evidence relating to base subject of the victim for its independence, corroboration, or refutation and present evidence in the following ways?

1. Independent evidence to prove a fact about a victim without corroboration about entities and activities.

2. Corroborating evidence to validate facts about a victim by using different evidence to prove the same facts in a base concept.

3. Refuting evidence to show countering facts about a victim.

C. Collective. Does the report show the investigator considered the total body of evidence in a case to determine victim's culpability in the following ways?

1. Rule out.

2. Rule in.

3. Deem exculpable.

4. Deem culpable.

III. Direction

A. Priorities. Does the report reflect the investigator sought to connect the victim and his actions to other scenes by evidence?

B. Status. Does the report meet the parameters to support the victim role, and determine the fact gaps?

C. Plans. Does the report outline the investigator's next step with the victim?

IV. Writing

A. Format. Does the report cover the victim and subordinate scenes by organizing the report in a logical order, making facts easy to find in four key areas of identifying the victim, detailing actions, explaining the outcomes of those actions, and statements?

B. Descriptions. Does the report describe the victim and the outcome with plain language detailing the head, and moving down the body, focusing on key parts and including subordinate scenes?

C. Grammar. Does the report use proper nouns and adjectives along with active verbs to show the victim as a person and his actions?

D. Style. Does the report cover the victim in the first person stating the facts in a clear and neutral manner?

4.5 EVALUATING WITNESS INVESTIGATIONS

The investigator evaluates the witness after the victim and before the suspect to parallel how the courts will shift from what happened to the victim to what the suspect did.

Goal. Did the investigator define the witness, and what the witness can contribute to the facts about the case?

I. Objectivity

A. Open Mindedness. Does the report reflect alternate ideas and courses of action from the information and evidence of witnesses?

B. Reasoning. Does the report show the investigator approached the witnesses and their evidence with logical thinking to prove ideas through facts?

C. Bias Awareness. Does the report show the investigator recognized potential bias with the witnesses?

II. Facts

A. Individual. Does the report show how to prove the witness's activities with the facts in the following ways?

1. Identify the witness?

2. The witness's presence by proximity and position.

3. The witness's interactions.

4. The witness's observations of possession or control by other entities.

5. Damage or injury connected with what the witness provides.

B. Group. Does the report validate facts by grouping similar evidence relating to base subject of the witness persons and information provided for its independence, corroboration, or refutation and present evidence in the following ways?

1. Independent evidence to prove a fact without corroboration.

2. Corroborating evidence to validate facts by using different evidence to prove the same facts.

3. Refuting evidence to show countering facts.

C. Collective. Does the report show the investigator considered the total body of evidence in a case to determine witness's indications of culpability in the following ways?

1. Rule out.

2. Rule in.

3. Deem exculpable.

4. Deem culpable.

III. Direction

A. Priorities. Does the report show the investigator sought to identify scenes and evidence from the witness?

B. Status. Does the report show the investigator assessed what the witnesses contributed and what they did not provide?

C. Plans. Does the report outline the investigator's next step with the witnesses who have provided evidence?

IV. Writing

A. Format. Does the report cover the witness by organizing it to cover the person's connection with the crime and any other persons involved, what the person knows, and what the person provides in the way of evidence?

B. Descriptions. Does the report describe the witness in detail and what the person adds to the investigation?

C. Grammar. Does the report use proper names, and active verbiage to cover the matter?

D. Style. Does the report cover the witness with factual neutrality in a clear first person style covering the facts in a flowing manner?

4.6 EVALUATING SUSPECT INVESTIGATIONS

The investigator evaluates the suspect last. The investigation must center on the suspect for court. This themed sub investigation comes at the culmination point of the investigation. All other themed sub investigations contribute to the suspect.

Goal. Did the investigator define the suspect, the suspect's actions, and how the suspect impacted the victim by the crime?

I. Objectivity

A. Open Mindedness. Does the report present evidence explaining why the investigator names a person suspect among many alternate possibilities?

B. Reasoning. Does the report show the investigator approached the suspect with logical thinking to prove facts through evidence?

C. Bias Awareness. Does the report show the investigator used evidence to maintain an unbiased approach beyond value judgments?

II. Facts

A. Individual. Does the report show how to prove the suspect's activities with the facts in the following ways?

1. The suspect's identity.

2. The suspect's presence.

3. The suspect's interactions.

4. The suspect's possession or control of other entities.

5. Damage or injury connected with the suspect's person or actions.

B. Group. Does the report validate facts by grouping similar evidence relating to base subject of the suspect for its independence, corroboration, or refutation and present evidence in the following ways?

1. Independent evidence to prove a fact about a suspect without corroboration.

2. Corroborating evidence to validate facts about a suspect by using different evidence to prove the same facts.

3. Refuting evidence to show countering facts about a suspect.

C. Collective. Does the report show the investigator considered the total body of evidence in a case to determine suspect culpability in the following ways?

1. Rule out a suspect.

2. Rule in a suspect.

3. Deem a suspect exculpable.

4. Deem a suspect culpable.

III. Direction

A. Priorities. Does the report reflect the investigator sought multiple areas of evidence to prove who did what?

B. Status. Does the report reflect how the evidence work meets the parameters for proving the suspect, and if the suspect work presents gaps of proof?

C. Plans. Does the report state the investigator's next moves regarding the suspect? The investigator recognizes if the suspect investigation needs more evidence and how to seek it.

IV. Writing

A. Format. Does the report cover the suspect and subordinate scenes by organizing the facts into sections identifying the suspect, detailing his actions, explaining the outcomes of those actions, and covering his statements if he made any?

B. Descriptions. Does the report describe the suspect in detail with plain language, including the attributed evidence? The report describes the suspect in an order from head to toe, focusing in on details.

C. Grammar. Does the report use language to make the suspect as a person and his actions clear?

D. Style. Does the report cover the suspect with factual neutrality in a clear first person style covering the facts in a flowing manner?

4.7 EVALUATING LAW INVESTIGATIONS

The report demonstrates the investigator's knowledge of the law and how the scenes and evidence relates to it. The law provides a standard for the investigator to examine the case against. The law investigation comes last. The next step for the case centers on whether the investigation can prove a person guilty in the eyes of the law.

Goal. Did the investigator define the law violations by connecting them with evidence to scenes, evidence, a victim, and a suspect?

I. Objectivity

A. Open Mindedness. Does the report show the application of all laws as possible to the case?

B. Reasoning. Does the report reflect logical thinking to prove laws through facts?

C. Bias Awareness. Does the report show fairness overcoming potential biases and using fact to apply the law?

II. Facts

A. Individual. Does the report show the laws applicable to the case, and how to prove them with the facts in the following ways?

1. Identify every entity involved.

2. Presence.

3. Interaction.

4. Possession or control.

5. Impact, damage or injury.

B. Group. Does the report validate facts by grouping similar evidence relating to base subject of the law for its independence, corroboration, or refutation and present evidence in the following ways?

1. Independent evidence to prove a fact about a law violation without corroboration about entities and activities.

2. Corroborating evidence to validate facts about entities and activities relating to law violations.

3. Refuting evidence to show countering facts about entities and activities relating to law violations.

C. Collective. Does the report show the investigator considered the total body of evidence in a case to determine culpability for the law violations in the following ways?

1. Rule out.

2. Rule in.

3. Deem exculpable.

4. Deem culpable.

III. Direction

A. Priorities. Does the report show the priorities of proving law violations with evidence?

B. Status. Does the report show the case includes enough evidence to charge a person with violating a law? Various levels of proof connect the laws and legal parameters with persons. Gaps in evidence, proof, and facts present opportunities to investigate more.

C. Plans. Does the report outline plans of what to do next with the laws comparing the status to the case priorities?

IV. Writing

A. Format. Does the report's format cover the laws in an organized way to make the alleged violations clear?

B. Descriptions. Does the report describe the elements of the law and add in the facts to describe the violation?

C. Grammar. Does the report use proper nouns and active verbs to cover the law and its elements overcoming long sentences, and passive verbiage complicating investigator writing?

D. Style. Does the report style explain the law violations in simple terms while removing the legalese and jargon?

CONCLUSION

The Decisive Investigator shows a method to solve cases, and what solving a case means from start to finish. By the end of a case the investigator has organized the investigation, worked scenes for evidence, worked the evidence for proof, and evaluated the proof of the investigation for facts proving who did what. The investigator passes the gathered body of facts to the next part of the justice system where a court can determine guilt or innocence.

A decisive investigator may build a limited collection of decisive facts, falling short of proving a suspect's guilt. Calling a person a suspect requires a little evidence, calling a person guilty requires a lot of it. Persons are innocent until proven guilty in court. A thorough investigation unable to prove guilt also protects against false convictions. Facts present many more options than the conclusions of guilty or not guilty. Unsolvable or unprovable cases are not failures but useful products of investigations providing facts to make good decisions.

The familiar oath in court to tell the truth, the whole truth, and nothing but the truth also applies to the report used to establish facts in a case. Of all the lessons from this book, the investigator should have refined the purpose of an investigation as not a simple quest to prove guilt, but to prove who did what by facts and find the truth.

INDEX

ABOUT THE AUTHOR

Eric Golembiewski served as a police officer, firefighter, and EMT in California for 15 years. He held positions of patrol officer, crime scene investigator, detective, fire investigator, trainer, and medic. Before investigative work, he served as a linguist and analyst in the Army. His classical education includes a BA in American Literature from the University of Arizona, and an MA in Liberal Arts with a Military History Concentration from Louisiana State University.

Made in United States
Orlando, FL
04 November 2026

90202250R00118